violence and aggression

HUMAN BEHAVIOR

violence and aggression

BY RONALD H. BAILEY
AND THE EDITORS OF TIME-LIFE BOOKS

TIME-LIFE BOOKS, NEW YORK

The Author: Ronald H. Bailey is a freelance author and journalist who was formerly a senior editor of LIFE. He is the author of another book in this series, *The Role of the Brain.* He has also published several articles on prison reform for the magazine *Corrections* and was a contributor to *The Unknown Leonardo,* a book about the inventive genius of Leonardo da Vinci. He and his wife and four children live on a farm in New York State.

General Consultants for Human Behavior:
Robert M. Krauss is Professor of Psychology at Columbia University. He has taught at Princeton and Harvard and was Chairman of the Psychology Department at Rutgers. He is the co-author of *Theories in Social Psychology,* formerly edited the *Journal of Experimental Social Psychology* and contributes articles to many journals on aspects of human behavior and social interaction.

Peter I. Rose, a specialist on racial and ethnic relations, is Sophia Smith Professor of Sociology and Anthropology at Smith College and is on the graduate faculty of the University of Massachusetts. His books include *They and We, The Subject is Race* and *Americans from Africa.* Professor Rose has also taught at Goucher, Wesleyan, Colorado, Clark, Yale, Amherst, the University of Leicester in England, Kyoto University in Japan and Flinders University in Australia.

James W. Fernandez is Professor of Anthropology at Princeton University. His field research has concentrated on cultural change in East, West and South Africa, and the Iberian peninsula. He has been President of the Northeastern Anthropological Association and a consultant to the Foreign Service Institute. He has also taught at Dartmouth College.

Special Consultant for Violence and Aggression:
Anthony N. Doob is Associate Professor of Psychology and Criminology at the University of Toronto. He is co-author of *Deviancy: The Psychology of Being Different,* co-editor of *Readings in Experimental Social Psychology,* and author of numerous articles on aggression. He is also editor of the *Journal of Experimental Social Psychology.*

Valuable help was given by the following departments and individuals of Time Inc.: Editorial Production, Norman Airey; Library, Benjamin Lightman; Picture Collection, Doris O'Neil; Photographic Laboratory, George Karas; TIME-LIFE News Service, Murray J. Gart; Correspondents Margot Hapgood and Dorothy Bacon (London), Ann Natanson and Deborah Sgardello (Rome), Maria Vincenza Aloisi (Paris), Elisabeth Kraemer (Bonn), S. Chang (Tokyo), Bernard Diederich (Mexico City), John Dunn (Melbourne), Barry Hillenbrand (Rio de Janeiro), James Shepherd (New Delhi), Bing Wong (Hong Kong).

HUMAN BEHAVIOR

Editorial Staff for *Violence and Aggression:*
EDITOR: William K. Goolrick
Text Editors: Betsy Frankel, Anne Horan
Picture Editor: Kathy Ritchell
Designer: John Martinez
Associate Designer: Marion Flynn
Staff Writers: Carol Clingan, Richard Cravens, Susan Hillaby, Suzanne Seixas
Chief Researcher: Ann Morrison
Researchers: Karen Bates, Oscar Chiang, Barbara Fleming, Tonna Gibert, Lea G. Gordon, Dunstan Harris, Beatrice Hsia, Catherine Ireys, Susan Jonas, Shirley Miller, Heidi Sanford, Ginger Seippel, Jane Sugden
Editorial Assistant: Janet Hubbard

Editorial Production
Production Editor: Douglas B. Graham
Assistant Production Editors:
Gennaro C. Esposito, Feliciano Madrid
Quality Director: Robert L. Young
Assistant Quality Director: James J. Cox
Associate: Serafino J. Cambareri
Copy Staff: Eleanore W. Karsten (chief), Susan B. Galloway, Eleanor Van Bellingham, Florence Keith, Pearl Sverdlin
Picture Department: Dolores A. Littles, Jessy Faubert
Traffic: Carmen McLellan

Contents

The Urge to Hurt

1

In London a young man is convicted of battering a Catholic priest to death with an ax, strangling one old woman and stabbing another. Jailed for life, he explains himself by saying that he "enjoyed killing." In a Chicago alley *(left)*, a boy raises his fist to strike his playmate. On the island of Bali, a tropical paradise that is renowned for its gentle, easygoing ways, political conflict leads to a blood bath. Before the violence has subsided, an estimated 40,000 people are killed, although the number may run as high as 80,000—as one observer said, "When people were killed in batches of less than ten, nobody even bothered to keep count."

Separated by thousands of miles, these episodes are noteworthy not because they are so unusual—they will soon be pushed out of memory by other, perhaps more savage, actions—but because they are so typical that they raise deeply disturbing questions. Is man violent by nature? That is, does he carry in his genes an inescapable drive to kill or harm his fellow man? Or is his violence learned, taught him by the examples and attitudes he sees in his society? If man is born violent, controlling such behavior may be virtually impossible. If, on the other hand, it is the product of learning and culture, there is hope, for the possibility exists that man can master his aggressions and save himself from self-destruction by applying those skills of learning and thinking that set him apart from other animals.

The study of aggression, perhaps more than any other aspect of human behavior, is studded with dilemma, anomaly, myth and just plain irony. There is, first of all, the human reaction to violence. People recoil from it, yet are drawn perversely to it—much like the child watching a horror movie who covers his eyes and cries, "I can't look!" —while all the time peering eagerly between his fingers. Crowds flock to scenes of violent tragedy, avid for every gory detail. Violent sports such as football and boxing draw millions of spectators. "We not only tolerate violence," the renowned psychiatrist Karl Menninger said, "we put it on the front pages of our newspapers. One-third or one-fourth of our television programs use it for the amusement of our children. Condone! My dear friends, we love it."

Moreover, aggression in its most virulent form—organized warfare—can evoke both the worst and the best of what it means to be human. A species that in wartime could perpetrate such atrocities as the extermination of six million Jews and the slaughter at My Lai could also muster the noblest of actions when confronted with a common enemy. Under siege during World War II, the British people were stimulated to great courage and self-sacrifice. Similarly, the international effort to defeat Fascism during the Spanish Civil War has been praised by the French author and intellectual André Malraux as "a most profound experience of brotherhood."

At quite a different level, aggression too often pays. Crime yields uncountable profits. The major powers of the world owe territorial possessions and influence to the force of arms. Aggressive behavior is the basis for the machismo that serves as a standard of conduct for young males in many Western societies. Even violent desperadoes like the British highwayman Dick Turpin and the American outlaw Jesse James won a fame that borders on idolatry.

Scientists and philosophers have been puzzling over these paradoxes for centuries, but it is only in recent years that systematic investigation has begun to suggest some answers. In laboratory experiments psychologists deliberately provoke aggression and then measure it. In field studies around the world, anthropologists study the cultures of peoples to whom violence is virtually unknown. In city streets sociologists mix with violent youth gangs to determine the causes and effects of antisocial behavior. Some of these experiments have proved highly controversial, and some have raised serious ethical questions. Certain experimenters have tampered with human behavior in dubious, possibly irresponsible ways—they have provoked unsuspecting people to anger, frustrated them or aroused and excited them in ways that could have resulted in serious physical or psychological injury to the subjects or to others. Yet whatever the questions raised by such experiments, the fact remains that once they had been conducted, they could not be ignored by students of human behavior.

The effort to unravel the mystery of violence and aggression bears a fateful significance, for the quality of human life and the survival of man are involved. Robbery, rape, riots, vandalism, marital strife, feuds with neighbors—all are part of the fabric of existence. In the late 1960s Americans were killing their fellow men at twice the rate of 20 years earlier, and the increase in murder was accompanied by an upsurge in rapes, muggings, burglaries and general destructiveness. Around the world, in cities once proud of their safe streets, violence soared. In London, violent crimes increased by 39 per cent in three years. In West Berlin, major crimes rose by a staggering 43 per cent in five years. And in Rome police calculated that thieves were striking at a rate of once every three and a half minutes. Even sports events and entertainment —books, films, television—became permeated with violence.

Almost as serious as the violence itself is the climate of fear that it engenders. A Gallup Poll conducted in the United States in 1972 found that 42 per cent of those interviewed were afraid to walk alone in the streets of their own neighborhoods at night. The fear prevailed even where the actual danger was slight. A reporter journeying through a peaceful rural area found the citizens of a small farm town aroused by the specter of crime and violence. Yet the community had not experienced a rape in 12 years or a murder in 21—and the only person in jail happened to be a 17-year-old arrested for reckless driving.

The climate of exaggerated fear was intensified by television's steady fare of violence—both real and make-believe. A survey conducted at the University of Pennsylvania revealed that TV viewers greatly overestimated the incidence of real-life violence in their own cities. The reason is easy to find: a half hour of television may carry in living color more acts of violence than the viewer will witness firsthand in the course of an entire lifetime.

One reason there is so much apprehension about violence and aggression is that there is so much misapprehension about them. Their nature, as much as their prevalence, is often misunderstood. Social scientists apply the term "aggression" to any behavior aimed at hurting another physically or emotionally. In this context, aggressive violence is behavior that is intended to injure a creature's own kind. Such a definition sharpens the view of the problem because it avoids questions raised by hunting. A wolf killing a caribou for supper is certainly violent, but it is no more guilty of aggression than the farm wife wringing the neck of a chicken. Similarly, man's propensity to hunt animals for food and sport—often cited as evidence of an innate love of killing—does not qualify as aggression.

The most dramatic examples of aggression—killing and physical attack—are obvious, of course. But words can also be vicious weapons, and expressions such as "tongue lashing" make clear the suffering inflicted by verbal aggression. The fact that aggression need not be

Man or woman, French (bottom right) or German (to left of Frenchman), every human expresses anger, according to psychologists

Paul Ekman and Wallace Friesen, with three universal signals: glowering eyes, knitted brows, and lips pursed or parted to shout.

physical leads to all sorts of ambiguities, however. The adjective "aggressive" is widely used to characterize behavior that does not create any problem for society. For example, a successful salesman may be called aggressive. He might better be termed assertive. Of course, by peddling his wares assertively he may cause his competitors psychic harm as a by-product. But he is not guilty of aggression unless he intends to harm them—or if he knowingly sells inferior merchandise, in which case he commits aggression against his customers.

Intent to cause harm is the crucial factor. The dentist, for example, does not qualify as an aggressor, although he knowingly causes pain. His intention is not to harm the patient. Similarly, the judge who condemns a murderer to the gallows or the policeman who uses reasonable force in subduing a criminal is not motivated by a desire to do harm but by the need to uphold law. And most societies sanction the use of physical punishment by parents to correct the misbehavior of their children.

As the problems of definition suggest, aggression is a complex process, one that must be understood on many different levels. To bring some semblance of order to it, psychologists tend to classify aggression in two general categories—emotional and instrumental—depending upon the ultimate aim of the behavior. Emotional aggression is reactive; it occurs in response to a particular provocation, pain, threat or frustration. These stimuli cause the brain and the chemical messengers known as hormones to order the heart to pump faster and send more blood with food and oxygen to the muscles. The palms sweat, the face flushes red with anger and, unless the emotional arousal is voluntarily controlled, an aggressive act is committed.

Anger need not be present in the second type of aggression, which takes place in cold blood. Here, aggression is the instrument for attaining a goal or a reward. The aggressor may be seeking money, status, territory, honor or simply his father's praise ("That's the way to stick up for yourself, Johnny!"). One of the most familiar forms of instrumental aggression is loyal obedience to the group, whether it be a street gang mobilizing for action or a nation calling its citizens to war in the name of patriotism.

The effort to pin down the causes of aggression—whether emotional or instrumental—has led men through the ages to blame witches, demons and the positions of the stars. In modern times, discoveries of science have been interpreted (or misinterpreted) to mean that physical defects are to blame, thereby giving society new scapegoats—mental disorders, bad genes and brain diseases. The notion that much of the world's mayhem might spring from measurable abnormalities somehow makes violence easier to live with.

The idea that genetic defects might be responsible for criminal violence was set forth early in the 19th Century by the Italian criminologist, Cesare Lombroso. This notion dies hard, although the evidence to support it can most charitably be described as controversial. It was revived recently by three Edinburgh psychologists in a study suggesting that an abnormality in the heredity units, or chromosomes, predisposes its bearer to antisocial behavior. Normal males each have one male and one female sex chromosome, while females have two female chromosomes. But about one boy in 1,000 is born with an extra male chromosome, and the Edinburgh study indicated that mentally defective men institutionalized for criminal behavior showed a higher prevalence of the extra chromosome than the general population. This abnormality was cited during the highly publicized trial of Richard Speck, the young maniac who murdered eight nurses in Chicago. As it turned out, Speck did not have the defect after all and the evidence against males who did could easily be attributed to another circumstance: they tend to be taller than average, and tall men are more likely to be singled out as the aggressor when policemen are called in to break up a fight.

Malfunctions of the brain also have been cast as the villains in violence. In the 1960s a team of Boston brain surgeons reported finding a high incidence of abnormal brain waves among prison populations. Their contention that brain disorders can cause violence received some support in the mad shooting spree of Charles Whitman in Austin, Texas, in 1966. After Whitman murdered his wife and mother, shot 38 persons from the top of a university tower and finally was gunned down himself, an autopsy revealed a huge tumor in his brain. But autopsies and medical examinations have shown that organic defects could, at most, account for only a negligible portion of human aggression. A broader explanation is needed. The oldest explanation holds that all human beings are born bad. This rationale is, of course, the doctrine of original sin, a concept that has survived even the scientific revolution and its rejection of many other religious values.

Ironically, the event that shook the foundations of most religions —Charles Darwin's statement of the theory of evolution—also provided new underpinnings for a secular version of original sin. Darwin believed that violence serves a useful purpose in the evolution of animals, by enabling the fittest—the best hunters and foragers—to survive.

Sunday Mirror

8p   October 5, 1975   No. 649

THIS VIOLENT SOCIETY

THE FACE of Britain is scarred with violence. Every day brings new acts of thuggery. Yesterday came reports of three more: The RAPE of a young girl by two men; the vicious MURDER by muggers of an innocent tradesman; an incredible ASSAULT by a human vampire on a terrified girl.

FIENDS RAPE AN AU PAIR

POLICE are hunting for two men who brutally raped an eighteen-year-old girl.

The rapists are also believed to have assaulted a young nurse.

And police think there may have been other unreported cases.

In both incidents the girls were picked up in London and driven to Dartford Heath, Kent—a favourite spot for courting couples.

The latest case, which came to light yesterday, involved a Danish au pair who lives in Hampstead.

She accepted a lift while waiting at a bus-stop in nearby St. John's Wood.

After getting into the car she was threatened. Her glasses were removed, and she was taken to the deserted heath.

The men dragged her into the undergrowth and the girl —said by police to have been a virgin—was raped by both attackers.

Same men

Detective Inspector Bernard Swift, who is leading the hunt, said he was sure the same men indecently assaulted a 23-year-old Malaysian nurse a month ago.

She was picked up in Oxford Street and taken to the heath—but escaped.

Police have appealed for other girls who may have suffered similar attacks to come forward.

'Vampire' in attack on girl of nine

A FIEND who made a vampire-style attack on a little girl of nine was being hunted by police yesterday.

C I D chief Bob Storey said: "It is vital we find this man to avoid a greater tragedy."

The attacker, wearing a stocking mask, leaped from bushes at the terrified girl who fell as she tried to escape.

The "vampire" bit her cheek, leaving a vicious wound, as she lay screaming.

The girl told police she saw blood on the man's mask and round his lips when he fled.

She was named as Tracey Robson, of Canon's Brook, Harlow, Essex. Her parents gave permission for her identity to be revealed to aid the hunt.

The attack happened near Tracey's home at Collins Meadow, Harlow.

Chief Inspector Storey, head of Harlow C I D, said: "It was one of the strangest we have known."

The "vampire" was said to be dressed in grey check trousers and a red sweater with thin black hoops.

GANG STABS Mr NICE GUY

THE reggae clubs and crowded cafes of London's Brixton were the scenes of a police murder hunt yesterday.

Their targets were a gang of vicious muggers who inflicted fatal stab wounds on fishmonger Edward Luder —a quiet, popular man.

He was pounced on by six youths, four black and two white, a few minutes after he had helped close up a fish shop in Brixton market on Friday evening.

He was driving in a van with his boss, Mr. Ruby Otto, and two other men carrying the day's takings from the shop.

The money had just been locked in the boot of 53-year-old Mr. Luder's car when they noticed that the tyres on a lorry belonging to Mr. Otto had been ripped.

It was while the men were looking at the damage that the gang attacked. Mr. Luder and his friends fought back fiercely. But he was stabbed three times—twice in the chest, once in an arm.

Then the attackers ran off, leaving the fish shop cash intact and Mr. Luder's lifeblood draining away.

Mr. Otto, 50, who was stabbed in the leg, drove him to hospital. But by midnight he was dead.

Mr. Luder's wife Annette, 45, of Glennie Road, Streatham, said later he was "a good father, a good husband and a good worker." He was also a tragic victim of our violent society.

'ARE YOU THE RAPIST?' Wife's question revealed—Page 5

BOND'S SECRET FILE

—PAGES 10, 11, 12 and 13

SLIMMING DRUG SHOCK

PAGE TWO

At the turn of the 20th Century, the application of Darwin's theory to human behavior became known as Social Darwinism, a philosophy holding that human progress would best be served by the survival of the fittest. The concept provided a handy pseudoscientific justification for acquisitive businessmen and war-lovers to pursue their interests with impunity. For example, the hero of the Spanish-American War, Colonel (later President) Theodore Roosevelt, justified war as a moral tonic. And in 1912, Prussian General Friedrich von Bernhardi found a receptive audience when he wrote: "War is a biological necessity. It is as necessary as the struggle of the elements in nature. . . . It gives a biologically just decision, since its decisions rest on the very nature of things."

The idea that aggression was a biological necessity found ready acceptance among the early practitioners of the new science of psychology. "Our ancestors have bred pugnacity into our bone and marrow," wrote psychologist William James. He believed there were "two souls" within man—"The one of sociability and helpfulness, the other of jealousy and antagonism to his mates."

In 1908 the British psychologist William McDougall called aggression "the instinct of pugnacity" and said it was probably the most important factor in man's evolution as a social being. To account for the differences in violence around the world, McDougall suggested that the strength of the instinct varied from race to race. White Europeans, for example, seemed to possess a stronger instinct for aggression than Asians, who were then assumed by Westerners to be peaceful. McDougall ignored the long history of murderous destruction in the Orient, and he could not foresee, of course, the Japanese aggression that would trigger World War II in Asia, the killing of a half million Moslems that accompanied the partition of India in 1947, or the slaughter of almost half a million Communists in Indonesia at the end of 1965 and the beginning of 1966.

The first to attempt a systematic explanation of aggression as an instinctive form of behavior was the father of psychoanalysis, Sigmund Freud. Though Freud had been trained as a physician and had engaged in considerable physiological research, his ideas about aggression grew principally from his experience with the troubled human mind. In Freud's early analyses of behavior, aggression did not play a primary role. The most important drive in man and animals, he believed, was the "life force" he called libido.

But after World War I, Freud's views changed in response to the turmoil he had witnessed in his own world—one that had been shaken to

15

Murder around the world

Although homicide is almost universal, an individual's chance of dying at another's hand varies greatly from country to country—as illustrated in the chart at right showing homicides per 100,000 from 1963 to 1972.

The homicide rate runs highest in the Western Hemisphere, where in countries such as Mexico, Venezuela and the United States cultural values emphasize violence, and guns are widely available. (The modest decrease in the Mexican and Venezuelan rates is attributed to a reduction in political violence.)

More typical of the industrialized nations are Japan and Norway, where stable, low levels of homicide prevail. Finland's unusually high rate has been blamed variously on the climate, isolation and Finnish drinking habits.

One night's harvest of fatal violence, both intentional and accidental, is recorded by a police photographer in the New York City morgue.

its foundations by the terrible destruction of the War. His new theory, like William McDougall's "instinct of pugnacity," postulated a second basic drive in opposition to the life force—an unconscious death wish. Freud called this drive Thanatos, from the Greek for "death." Turned inward, it resulted in the masochistic desire to hurt oneself and, in extreme cases, to commit suicide. Directed outward, it became aggression.

Freud's new view of "an active instinct for hatred and destruction" was set forth in 1932 in a celebrated letter to Albert Einstein, who had been asked by the League of Nations to initiate a dialogue with other scientists on an important problem of the time. Einstein, whose brilliant work in physics would one day lead to the ultimate weapons of violence, nuclear bombs, chose as his topic: "Is there any way of delivering mankind from the menace of war?"

Freud's answer was exceedingly pessimistic. "There is no use in trying to get rid of man's aggressive inclinations," he wrote. "Wars will only be prevented with certainty if mankind unites in setting up a central authority to which the right of giving judgment upon all conflicts of interest shall be handed over. We shall be making a false calculation if we disregard the fact that law was originally brute violence and that even today it cannot do without the support of violence."

In his other writings, Freud did offer a measure of hope. Aggression had to have an outlet, he suggested, but it could find this outlet in several ways. One way was the direct expression of anger. A second was the displacement or redirection of destructive energy to a target other than the one that had aroused aggressive emotions. Such a substitute target might be inanimate—the aggressor would kick a can and not the family dog. A third outlet was sublimation, the process by which antisocial impulses are rechanneled toward constructive ends, finding expression in political activity, scientific explorations, the performance of useful labor or even the creation of works of art.

Although doubts have been cast on these concepts by later psychological experiments, Freud's ideas are still widely held. Many psychoanalysts subscribe to his notion that aggression is innate and that a failure to express, displace or sublimate aggressive impulses can bring on neurosis, psychosomatic ailments and even serious mental illness.

Modern acceptance of the theory of innate aggression, however, owes less to Freud and his disciples than to several books that depict man as aggressive by nature. The most influential books were *On Aggression*, by the distinguished Austrian scientist Konrad Lorenz, and *African Genesis* and *The Territorial Imperative*, by Robert Ardrey, who popularized studies by a number of authorities. These authors relied heavily on re-

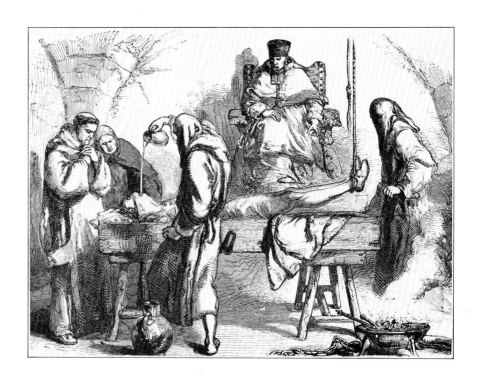

cent observations of animal behavior in reaching their conclusions.

Lorenz, a noted but controversial zoologist and ethologist, became the chief authority for this view of human nature. He maintained in his books that animals display a variety of aggressive behavior, but that they usually stop short of killing their own kind. Some species are indeed ferocious. For example, the aptly named Siamese fighting fish will attack others of its own species on sight. In a laboratory tank it quickly learns to swim through a plastic ring if its pugnacity is rewarded by the sight of a dummy made up like another Siamese or even if it sees a mirror that flashes back its own image. But as animals move up the evolutionary ladder toward man, claimed Lorenz, the fighting tends to be formalized into relatively nonhazardous rituals that rarely lead to serious injury; he maintained that fighting aimed at killing an opponent appeared to be practically nonexistent.

The gorilla hoots, beats its chest, bares its dagger-like canine teeth and thumps the ground with its hand. But in spite of this fearsome show, the gorilla is a comparatively placid vegetarian that, unlike its distant human cousin, rarely kills anything.

Lorenz suggested three functional reasons why nature may have armed animals with an instinct for aggression. Most vertebrates—animals with a backbone—apparently fight their own kind for sex, territory or dominance, wrote Lorenz. Because animals fight about sex, Lorenz said, in many species the strongest male gets the most desirable female. As Darwin pointed out, this result helps to assure that future generations inherit the stronger, more adaptive features of the victor.

The second function of animal aggression, according to Lorenz, is to provide each individual sufficient space to ensure an ample food supply. Animals stake out a claim and stand ready to fight for it, behavior that is known as territoriality. Different animals mark their home ground in various ways. Birds sing out a warning when trespassers come too close to their nests; dogs and wolves mark their territorial borders with deposits of urine or feces; and coral fish warn off others by their flamboyant colors. An animal's territory may be as small as a woodpecker's nesting tree or as large as the nine-mile-wide range necessary to sustain a family of wolves. The farther an animal happens to be from the center of its territory, the less likely it is to fight. In some battles an observer can easily predict the winner—the fighter that is nearer to its home ground.

Territoriality does not always involve a static piece of real estate. Starlings, for example, maintain a carefully prescribed distance from one another—something like the "personal space" humans seem to need around them. The starlings' need for individual space accounts for the strikingly regular pattern formed by a flock perched on a telephone wire, strung out at uniform intervals like pearls. When the starlings first land on the wire, they may bunch up, but soon the crowded ones begin to peck at one another until they are separated by the proper distance—precisely a peck of the beak away.

The third reason for aggression in animals, according to Lorenz, is the establishment and maintenance of dominance structures, social hierarchies rife with human parallels. The study of dominance in animals began in 1913, when the Danish zoologist Thorleif Schjelderup-Ebbe became intrigued by the bickering and squabbling in his hen coop. He quickly discovered that what appeared to be random fighting fitted neatly into a pattern. The hens had established an order of status in which each knew its place. When a strange hen was introduced into the coop, it started competing for food with the others, a dispute that was finally settled with squawks, flapping wings and vigorous pecking. Hens that gave way to the stranger acknowledged its superiority, while those that forced the stranger away from food established their superiority. The ranking was finely divided, Schjelderup-Ebbe discovered. Each hen had its own position in the pecking order—it could peck any hen below it and could be pecked by any hen above it.

The unshakable power of the pecking order was demonstrated in experiments in which the male sex hormone testosterone was given to hens

The paradox of Japanese violence

Everyone everywhere has a potential for violence or nonviolence, but nowhere has this split in human nature seemed more vividly paradoxical—at least to Westerners—than in Japan.

The Japanese are generally considered a courteous, hard-working people who delight in such gentle pursuits as the cultivation of the perfect chrysanthemum and the enjoyment of the elaborately polite tea ceremony. They are also capable of terrible brutality. Their most popular national epic is the *Forty-Seven Ronin*, a tale of samurai who avenge their leader's death by beheading his enemy *(below)*. And it is the Japanese who invented the hara-kiri ceremony of disembowelment and the ritualized assassination *(right)*, in which the killer stabs a political leader and later turns the sword on himself.

In a painting of a famous Japanese epic of the early 18th Century, 47 samurai break into the house of the lord whose treachery caused the death of their leader. After slicing off the traitor's head they kill themselves—an act of violence acclaimed by their countrymen.

Eyeglasses awry and face distorted, Socialist Party Chairman Inejiro Asanuma recoils from a fatal stab wound as his 17-year-old assassin prepares to deliver a second blow. This horrifying scene took place before an audience of 3,000 at a rally in 1960. The assassin committed suicide—as Japanese tradition required—while in prison awaiting trial.

that ranked low in dominance. Testosterone tends to make certain animals more aggressive and, accordingly, the experimental hens got tough when cooped up with strangers. But when they were put back with their own flocks, the hens automatically resumed their low status and made no attempt to challenge their superiors.

Scientists now know that dominance hierarchies exist in many vertebrate species and offer several advantages from an evolutionary standpoint. Among baboons, for example, a system of dominance enables the strongest males to take over defense of the troop. When a baboon troop roams in search of food, the dominant males normally stay in the middle of the group, standing guard over the mothers and the very young. But if an external threat, such as a leopard or a human hunter, is detected by the younger males around the perimeter of the troop, the leaders leave their central position and array themselves in a defensive semicircle in front of the troop.

Dominance also provides a stable social structure. Well-ordered societies probably are better equipped to compete for evolutionary survival. And even though dominance sparks fighting in the process of setting up the pecking order, it later acts to help prevent destructive fighting. Boss baboons, for example, appear to serve the function of policemen in the troop, breaking up fights among the young and generally keeping the peace.

This conciliatory aspect of dominance represents one instance of the phenomenon that Lorenz and other ethologists considered most significant about aggression in the animal kingdom—the existence of inhibitions against deadly violence. Some of these controls are built into the physical characteristics of the species. Animals have fangs, claws and tusks, but few are sufficiently armed to destroy adversaries of their own kind the way a man can kill another human with a single stab of a dagger. Even when an animal possesses an unusually deadly weapon, there may be built-in protective devices to limit its destructiveness. Rattlesnakes are immune to their own venom; when fighting each other they have to engage in a kind of harmless and unwieldy wrestling.

The most extraordinary inhibition resides in the quality of mercy shown by animals. They often fight until the issue is decided; then they stop and the loser departs, hurt perhaps but seldom seriously so. The trigger for this apparent act of chivalry is the willingness of the defeated opponent to flash a gesture of appeasement—in effect, a hands-up sign of surrender. Some animals surrender by showing the rump, others by cowering, bowing down or crouching. The defeated wolf turns its head and offers the victor the most vulnerable place on his body, the jugular vein at the side of the neck. One bite there would kill, but invariably the gesture itself satisfies the victor.

Lorenz maintained that aggression in human beings is also instinctive. What makes it more destructive than animal aggression, he wrote, is the lack of built-in inhibitors against the terrible weapons man has developed. If men fought only with their fists and natural strength, the fighting usually would be halted short of killing by such natural inhibitors as pain and physical exhaustion, or by the use of appeasement signals. But the great problem of man's aggressiveness is that he has developed terrible weapons against which natural inhibitors and appeasement are often ineffective. The weapons have come so fast that evolution has not been able to keep pace.

Increasingly complex weapons, Lorenz maintained, make violence among humans increasingly a remotely controlled activity—the aggressor may never even see his victim, preventing the effective operation of whatever moral controls evolution might have instilled in man. "The deep, emotional layers of our personality simply do not register the fact that the crooking of the forefinger to release a shot tears the entrails of another man," said Lorenz.

What makes Lorenz so controversial is not just his contention that aggression is innate, though that alone is hotly disputed. Lorenz insisted that the expression of aggressive instincts is inevitable; aggression can build up uncontrollably and then erupt spontaneously. Most authorities disagree. In their view, aggressive behavior requires a trigger, in animals as well as in humans. Animals become aggressive only in response to an external stimulus. In man, too, a stimulus is needed to arouse and trigger aggression, but the stimuli are more varied than those setting off animals and their effect is heavily influenced by learning. The explosion is seldom spontaneous and is not inevitable.

Lorenz, in effect, likened aggression to water or steam rising in a sealed container. Unless the pressure is drained off, the container springs a leak or explodes. Similarly, said Lorenz, aggressive energy mounts in the nervous systems of humans and animals and must be drained off somehow or the organism simply explodes. For this reason Lorenz' theory is known as the hydraulic model of aggression (some psychologists refer to it irreverently as the flush-toilet model).

The hydraulic model places man in a precarious situation; it means that he has an aggressive instinct so powerful that it could bring about his destruction. Lorenz refused to believe that such a dismal outcome is inevitable, holding instead that human intelligence should be able to

Finding insights in the funny side of violence

Cartoonists have long mined a rich vein of humor in the aggression and hostility, some expressed, some not *(below)*, that form an inevitable part of everyday experience. What they draw not only focuses attention on the natural foibles of humanity but also reveals much about the nature of aggression.

The *Punch* cartoon at left illustrates the common compulsion to return offenses tit for tat, and it also shows one source of hostility: invasion of personal territory, whether by a tree limb or a shirt sleeve. And the sequence at right gives a sharply accurate description of the "displacement of aggression," the process of taking out anger on an innocent bystander, particularly one who cannot fight back.

"I hate everybody, regardless of race, creed, or place of national origin!"

Drawing by Peter Arno; © 1952 The New Yorker Magazine, Inc.

Drawing by Chas. Addams; © 1956 The New Yorker Magazine, Inc.

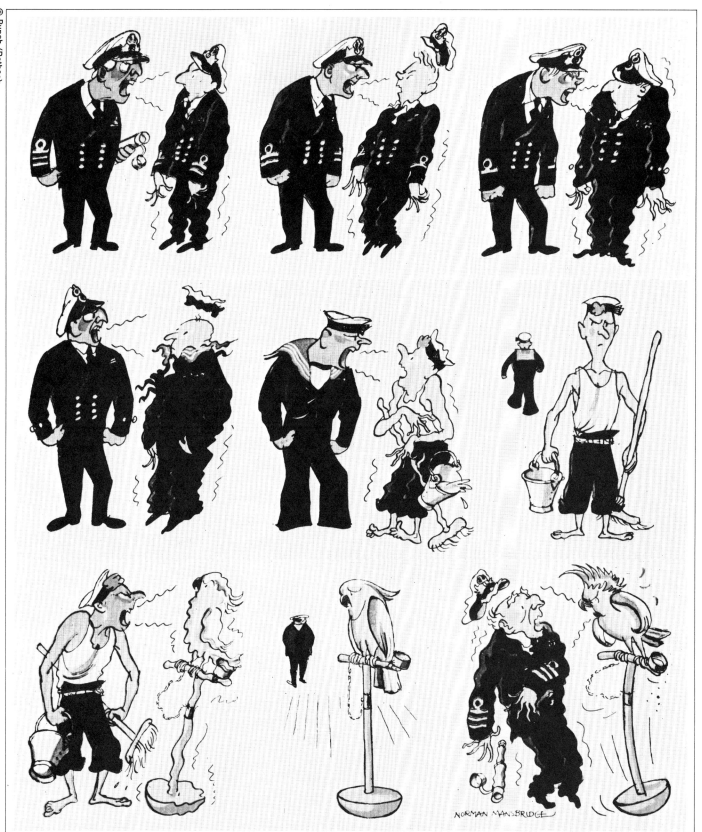

A cycle of displaced aggression aboard a British ship goes full circle, commander to parrot to commander, in this English cartoon sequence.

find ways of diverting aggression into harmless channels. But he tempered this hope with a blunt assessment of present prospects: "An unprejudiced observer from another planet," he wrote, "looking upon man as he is today, in his hand the atom bomb, the product of his intelligence, in his heart the aggression drive inherited from his anthropoid ancestors, which this same intelligence cannot control, would not prophesy long life for the species."

This despondent assessment of human behavior is disputed not only by psychologists, whose research on people argues against an inborn drive to violence, but also by other experts on animals. In particular, specialists in a field called sociobiology, the systematic study of the biological basis of behavior patterns, believe that animal habits differ in significant ways from the pictures presented by Lorenz, and that these differences undermine his dire conclusions.

The case of the sociobiologists was presented most eloquently by Edward O. Wilson of Harvard, who came along after Lorenz and had the benefit of new information. Wilson flatly disagreed with his predecessor. "The case for a pervasive aggressive instinct does not exist," Wilson said. The key word is "pervasive." Wilson took exception to the view that all animals share the instinct for aggression. Animal behavior is much more varied and more complex than that, he wrote. Some animals are pacific, nonaggressive creatures. Often they act altruistically, even sacrificing their own lives for the good of their fellows. Ants, bees and wasps will defend their colonies with suicidal attacks. Dolphins will gather together to help a stricken comrade by pushing it up to the surface of the water where it can breathe more easily. Elephants will try desperately to revive a dying comrade *(page 29)*.

Other animals may be pacific until threatened, and still others regularly exhibit extremely aggressive behavior, which even includes killing their own kind. Animal aggression, according to Wilson, is not always as inhibited by ritual as Lorenz indicated. Ants conduct "assassinations, skirmishes and pitched battles," he noted, adding: "Recent studies of hyenas, lions and langur monkeys, to take three familiar species, have disclosed that under natural conditions these animals engage in lethal fighting, infanticide and even cannibalism at a rate far above that found in human beings."

Such facts, accumulated largely in the great expansion of wild animal investigations of recent decades, suggest that environment—the situation—determines animal behavior as it does human behavior. The capacity for violence may be inborn, but its expression in overt behavior depends on many more factors than genetic inheritance. It is not inevitable. Wilson, in rejecting the hydraulic model of aggression, wrote that he knows of no evidence that man's aggressiveness "constitutes a drive searching for an outlet. Certainly the conduct of animals cannot be used as an argument for the widespread existence of such a drive." He maintained: "The key is the environment. What the genes prescribe is not necessarily a particular behavior but the capacity to develop certain behaviors and more than that, the tendency to develop them in various specified environments."

Scientists are sharply divided on the value of animal studies. Animal behavior specialists believe they are an illuminating guide to human behavior, while many psychologists discount their value. There are obvious parallels, however. The three reasons for animal aggression cited by Lorenz—sex, dominance and territory—apply to human beings as well. Men have fought in their backyards and on a global scale for territory and dominance, and sex need hardly be mentioned as a source of conflict. But men are much more complicated than animals, and their motivations in killing, maiming or insulting fellow members of their species are more varied. As one psychologist put it, "Animals don't fight over politics or religion."

Yet even if the parallels with animals are disregarded, there is strong evidence that man's violence is at least partly innate, an essential part of human nature. The plain fact that aggression is a male characteristic is one indication.

Over most of the world boys are more aggressive than girls—verbally, physically and even in their fantasies. Young boys are the ones who do the pushing and shoving, and the pattern becomes so firmly fixed early in life that many scientists consider violence largely a male problem. For the most part, men fight the wars, engage in aggressive crimes and commit the murders. In the United States, four of every five homicides and nine of every 10 robberies are the work of males.

Violence is such an ingrained preoccupation of males that they even seem to perceive its presence more readily than females. One way to demonstrate this difference in the laboratory is to flash two different pictures simultaneously on a stereoscope, a device that sends one image to one eye, the other image to the other eye. Since the brain cannot handle two totally different images simultaneously, it usually ignores one—if the test subject is asked what he sees, he will report a view of one picture or of the other but not of both. The "neutral" picture may show a mailman; the other shows a man with a dagger in his back. Not only do males tend to report seeing the violent image more often, the tendency

Gentle, deadly world of animals

Animals were long believed to be less aggressive than men. While they engaged in violent behavior, killing other species, it was thought that they stopped short of killing their own kind. Recent evidence, however, indicates that animal behavior is far more varied—and deadly—than previously believed.

At one end of the spectrum, according to Edward Wilson of Harvard, animals can be extremely altruistic—elephants have been photographed trying to rescue a comrade in distress *(far right)*. At the other end, animals are also capable of the most vicious forms of aggression, including the murder of their own kind, Wilson reported. Compared with animals, he concluded, "human beings are well down the list of aggressive creatures."

In vicious combat, lions in Nairobi National Park, Kenya, slug it out toe to toe. The fight between these animals was started by the lion on the right, and ended when the other animal lost an eye.

In a massive show of animal altruism, elephants in an African preserve vainly try to revive a dying cow.

to see it increases in age with both men and women. This suggests that as people grow older they learn and experience more about violence and tend to expect its presence. (Women can also be taught by their culture to be more like men—and thus more aggressive. In recent years violent crimes by females have increased relative to the male crime incidence, a change attributed by some authorities to the leveling of sex distinctions brought about by the women's liberation movement.)

The fact that there is such a sharp sex difference in aggressiveness —it is never totally eradicated in any culture—indicates it must be controlled by a physical trait that is set, like eye color, by genes borne on the sex chromosome. But apart from the sex difference, there is little evidence of genetically determined aggressive behavior.

Moreover, physiological evidence, piling up in recent years, refutes the idea that all violent behavior is programed in the human genes. This evidence comes mainly from new knowledge about the brain. It shows that the capacity for violence, the inborn ability to react violently, is located in "aggression centers" deep within the brain. Brain scientists, by cutting away certain portions of these areas, can make a vicious monkey unable to fight. Similarly, they can turn on rage and aggression by inserting miniature electrodes in the aggression center and switching on a slight electrical current. Brain stimulation of this kind also has been demonstrated in humans, who were made to feel angry, euphoric and even sexy by electrical currents sent to brain centers known as the amygdala, thalamus and hypothalamus.

While the brain stimulation experiments make clear that some capacity for aggression is innate in all creatures, they also show that the exercise of this capacity is not preordained. The potential for the behavior is built in, but the behavior is not; whether it will appear depends upon a complex of other factors. What happens when aggression centers are electrically stimulated hinges upon previous experience, the situation and the nature of the target. The interpretation of these environmental factors is directly controlled by the higher centers of the brain and has little to do with biological instinct. A pioneer in brain stimulation experiments, José Delgado, described experiments at Yale University in which a monkey was electrically stimulated. It became agitated, yet it would not attack a "boss monkey," one that it had previously learned was its superior in the colony's pecking order.

The biologist J. P. Scott concluded: "There is no physiological evidence of any spontaneous stimulation for fighting arising within the body. This means that there is no need for fighting, either aggressive or defensive, apart from what happens in the external environment. We may conclude that a person who is fortunate enough to exist in an environment which is without stimulation to fight will not suffer physiological or nervous damage because he never fights. We can also conclude that there is no such thing as a simple 'instinct for fighting' in the sense of an internal driving force which has to be satisfied." Many animals, it is now clear, have to learn to be aggressive and even to be predators. The famous lioness Elsa, of the book and movie *Born Free*, was raised as a household pet in Africa and had to be taught to hunt before it could take its place in the wild.

Man, above all others, is the learning animal. Whatever his innate potentialities, his aggressive behavior—and all of "human nature"—is shaped largely by his experience of the world, by the values of his culture and by the specific situations that he is thrust into. One token of this truth is the way the level of violence varies markedly from culture to culture and from country to country. In some societies violence is practically nonexistent—the Tasaday Indians of the Philippines do not even have a word for war. And between two industrially advanced nations such as the United States and England, radical differences are apparent. The Manhattan borough of New York City has more murders annually than England and Wales combined, although they have 30 times Manhattan's population. No theory of instinctive, inborn aggression can account for such differences.

The argument over aggression as a human instinct may never be settled to everyone's satisfaction. Perhaps the final word on the subject belongs to a nonscientist, the long-time American leader of socialist and pacifist causes, Norman Thomas, who wondered why, if war is so instinctive, governments have to draft men into military service and then threaten them with the firing squad if they desert.

Rituals of aggression

Most societies—ancient and modern, in every part of the world—have evolved rituals of aggression: socially approved public spectacles in which combatants vie in elaborate displays of physical violence. They may attack each other like gladiators or prize fighters, inflict pain on themselves, stage battles or even smash up automobiles.

In its purest form, the ritual of aggression is a sham battle, like that on page 38, in which opposing sides go through the motions of real warfare while observing regulations that limit injuries. All of the rituals involve action that seems aggressive to outsiders, but are such an accepted part of the societies in which they occur that the pain and the physical violence are ignored.

In every form such rituals attract appreciative audiences, for all are engrossing entertainments. Psychologists speculate that an important reason for their popularity is that they arouse excitement and thus satisfy the strong need almost everyone has for mental stimulation. Because they are conducted according to rules, the violence is kept in check and prevented from developing into full-scale destruction.

Such observations lead many authorities to believe that ritualized aggression is an essential safety valve, giving participants and spectators an opportunity to work out aggressiveness in relatively harmless ways. But this view of the cathartic value of the rituals is challenged by evidence that participation in violence, whether active or vicarious, controlled or not, adds fuel to the fires of aggression *(Chapter 5)*—and that organized violence makes people more aggressive rather than less.

Frantically flailing one another in a writhing mass of aggression, Japanese youths clad only in loin cloths scramble for a few sticks thrown in their midst. At the climax of this purification rite, a boy retrieving a stick wins 100,000 yen.

33

Self-inflicted suffering

Among the oldest forms of ritualized aggression are those in which celebrants mutilate or flog their own bodies in religious ceremonies. Above, hooded Christian penitents wind through an Italian village, raking nail-studded cork pads over their bare, bloody chests.

Carrying out what they believe are the wishes of a malevolent deity, Queen of the Witches, Balinese dancers draw blood by stabbing themselves with flame-shaped daggers called krisses.

Man against man—or woman

Some rites of aggression pit individuals against each other in contests designed to test strength and endurance. At left, two men of the Waurá tribe of the upper Amazon grapple in a muscle-straining wrestling match. According to some anthropologists, such staged struggles serve as a substitute for other kinds of violence between members of the tribe.

Hoping to prove her mettle as a prospective wife, a girl of the Hamar tribe in southwestern Ethiopia taunts a boy as he whips her. Her ability to endure the whipping successfully will earn her the privilege of marrying into his clan.

Formalized aggression between groups often imitates warfare on a limited scale. Above, men of New Guinea's Dani tribe, following a custom since outlawed by the government, go into a ritualized battle. They stay at least 50 feet apart and use defective arrows—still some were killed.

In a rugby "scrum" (right), one of the roughest of all modern sports encounters, two packs of forwards shove furiously as they strive to get at the ball (bottom center). The players are protected by nothing more than low boots, socks, shorts and jerseys, making bone-crushing injuries a fairly frequent occurrence.

Group versus group

Machines battling machines

A new dimension is given to violence in the "demolition derby," a form of motorized madness in which a car serves as an instrument of aggression. In the noisy heat of the early stages of a derby (right), contestants weave in and out, banging into one another while trying to avoid being put out of action themselves. They continue deliberately smashing their automobiles until only one is left operative, battered but still running.

Lessons in Aggression

2

Among the Yanomamö tribesmen of southern Venezuela, aggression and violence are a way of life. Above all other values, these primitive people put a premium on *waiteri*—ferocity. The nurture of *waiteri* begins at the moment of birth: if the newborn is a girl, and thus not suitable to become a warrior, the mother may kill her. As anthropologist Napoleon Chagnon noted, this sex-biased infanticide continues a vicious cycle. There is already a chronic shortage of women and the pirating of women provokes new battles in on-again, off-again warfare between villages of the tribe.

Chagnon's adventures among the Yanomamö provide a rare glimpse of how the nurture of aggressive values can affect an entire culture. Like infants everywhere, Yanomamö youngsters express their aggressive feelings freely. But their parents, instead of teaching the young to control their anger, encourage them to vent it over the most trivial incidents. They tease the toddler to arouse his *waiteri* and then laugh approvingly when he strikes out at them. The father, in particular, sets an example of brutality, cruelty and treachery. When he is not fighting tribesmen of other villages or exchanging blows with a neighbor, he is apt to be beating his wife with a stick of firewood or burning her with a glowing coal. Young Yanomamö boys practice endlessly the warrior role they were born into. They memorize death speeches to be uttered if they are mortally wounded and even rehearse the agony of combat—a different groan for each part of the body an enemy arrow might pierce.

To be sure, the Yanomamö culture has more benign characteristics than these. Many men form lifelong friendships. A woman's brothers defend her against a husband who outdoes himself in cruelty, and her sons-in-law will take care of her when she is old. By such checks and balances, the Yanomamö society holds together—but at a cost of many slashed limbs and burn scars, constant upheaval and a psychic disposition to mistrust practically everyone.

Several thousand miles to the north is the arid homeland of the Hopi

Indians, whose behavior is almost the opposite of the Yanomamö's—or was until recent times. A Hopi boy could not imagine punching his father —or anyone else—for neither his father nor any member of the community was likely to raise his hand against another. Children were gentled—spoiled by Western standards—and adults were seldom subjected to more than sharp words. The Hopi did get angry but rarely fought. There were no Hopi warriors and usually no wars, though the tribes defended their villages valiantly when attacked by other people.

Peoples whose behavior is as divergent as the Yanomamö and Hopi are to be found on every continent, in every racial group and cultural type. The bushmen of Africa's Kalahari Desert are hunter-gatherers like the Yanomamö but are no more violent than Hopi farmers; nearby in southern Africa live the Zulu, aggressive pastoral people who in past years were always at war with their neighbors. Such striking differences are not limited to those who still try to live in ancient ways. The world's most highly industrialized nation, the United States, is also one of the world's most violent—its murder rate, a reliable indicator, is among the highest recorded—94 out of every one million people were murdered in a single year. Yet Great Britain, homeland of the ancestors of many Americans, has been notable for its lack of violence; its murder rate is one seventh the rate in the United States.

The existence of such striking contradictions convinces most experts that vicious behavior is not simply an inherent flaw in human nature, a genetically directed activity like breathing. If it were, it would be more or less uniform around the world. Since it is not uniform, but varies with culture, it must be learned in the same way other aspects of culture are learned. Some psychologists believe violence is not genetically directed at all but is entirely learned; they think it is no more inborn than the ability to write. Most scientists take a middle view, maintaining that human inheritance brings some tendency toward expressing emotions in violence, but that this tendency is of slight importance, for it can be either suppressed or developed by society; thus how violently a person behaves depends almost entirely on how violently he was taught to behave.

The belief that violence is learned is supported by experiments conducted in many countries. They indicate that, beginning in childhood, human beings are taught to be as violent as their culture demands in the same ways they are taught the speech or table manners of their society. They learn through imitation, picking up behavior patterns they see around them, and also through the general process called conditioning, in which rewards and punishments—some obvious, some subtle—influence the development of certain types of behavior. Both imitation and conditioning begin in the home, but they are greatly influenced by the broader world outside—by schools, national traditions and religion, as well as by books, magazines, newspapers, and especially movies and television, as is demonstrated by the children imitating TV violence on page 42. The mechanisms interplay with one another, often overlapping and sometimes seeming contradictory, and it is difficult to extract one from the others in explaining violent and aggressive behavior. Insofar as they can be isolated, the process seems to begin with imitation. And how effectively children engage in imitation has been demonstrated by some controversial experiments by Stanford University psychologist Albert Bandura.

Bandura chose as his laboratory the nursery school—a place that normally bustles with what seems to be spontaneous pushing and shoving, temper tantrums and tussles for favorite toys. He chose as a target for childish aggression a four-foot-high inflatable doll called Bobo the Clown, a toy that is meant to be pushed and punched: it is weighted at the bottom so that every time it is struck, it pops back up for more.

In the simplest of the Bobo experiments, Bandura divided his subjects into three groups. One group spent 10 minutes in a room watching an adult, a member of the research team who served as a "model" the children might be expected to imitate. The model attacked the Bobo doll by punching its nose, hitting it over the head with a mallet and finally sitting on the resilient doll—all the while accompanying his actions with such exclamations as "Sockeroo!" and "Stay down!" The second group of children saw the same model play quietly with a construction toy. Afterward, these children and those from the third group, who had been given no preparation of any kind, were taken individually to a room where there was a Bobo doll and a variety of toys. The children who had been exposed to the aggressive behavior copied the model and attacked Bobo. The children of the other two groups played amiably with the toys—and with Bobo, which they pushed and wrestled in a friendly fashion but seldom attacked.

In the simple Bobo doll experiment the aggressive model existed in the flesh. But what if the model is not real and instead is a fantasy character projected in film or on the TV screen? Albert Bandura and his Stanford group found out by using the Bobo doll. This time their nursery school subjects were divided into five groups. As in the previous experiment, one group observed the antics of an aggressive model, a second group watched a nonaggressive model and a third group saw no

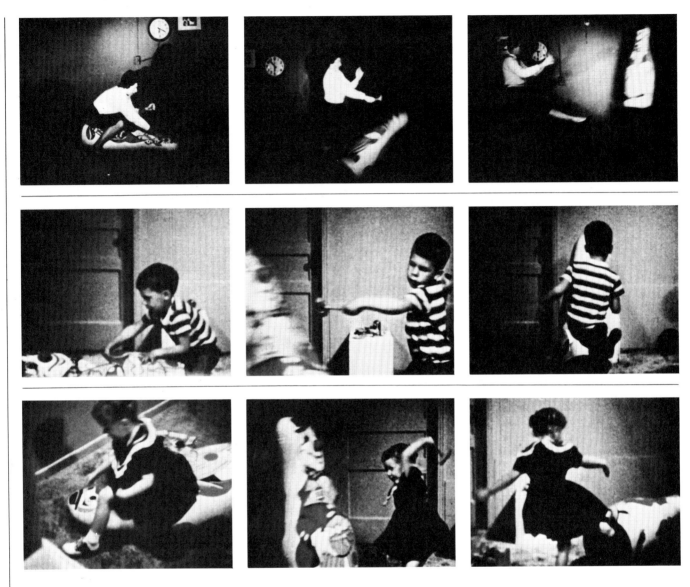

model at all. In addition, another group was shown a color film of the aggressive model pummeling Bobo. And a fifth group saw a cartoon-like film of the model, costumed as a cat, who attacked Bobo against a fantasy backdrop of brightly colored trees and butterflies.

Whether the aggressive model was seen in the flesh or in the fantasy of film did not seem to matter to the children. In fact, the ones who had seen the films were even more belligerent afterward than the children who had observed the real-life aggressive model. The researchers were able to distinguish two separate types of aggressive behavior. As before, the children showed distinctly new ways of attacking the Bobo doll, which they had learned from watching the aggressive model in person or on film. But watching the model also had apparently led them to act out aggressive behavior already in their repertoire. They spanked dolls, smashed toy cars and played at shooting plastic animals. None of these acts had been performed by the aggressive model in person or on film. Watching such a model, the researchers concluded, not only teaches new ways of aggression—it also somehow increases the tendency to behave aggressively.

Bandura and his colleagues have performed similar experiments in a host of permutations: with models attacking each other instead of Bobo; with models being rewarded with sweets for their aggression in some instances, being punished in other instances and reaping no consequences at all in still others; with the model under attack behaving abjectly in some instances and retaliating in others; and, in all these combinations, with some children watching the models in the flesh and others watching them on film.

No matter what the variations, the Bobo experiments showed again and again that the children did as they saw the models do. When the model kicked, the children kicked. When the model hammered, the children hammered. When the model exclaimed "Sockeroo!" the children exclaimed "Sockeroo!"

These experiments are direct proof only of immediate imitation; but imitation is, of course, learning by example and it undoubtedly helps to establish an enduring pattern of behavior. Other experiments suggest that the effect is indeed long lasting. In 1968, David J. Hicks of California State University did a variation on the Bobo doll experiments, using films of children and adults fighting each other. He found that eight months after very young children saw the films of violent behavior, they still retained 40 per cent of the aggressive ways they had learned from the models, even though they were not exposed to them after the first trial.

Even more convincing evidence of long-range effects—because it was gathered over a considerable span of time—came from an investigation of a group of 875 children living in a rural district of New York State. Psychologist Leonard Eron first studied the children when they were about eight years old. He asked each of them a series of questions about himself and his classmates: "Who starts a fight over nothing?" "Who is always getting into trouble?" "Who says mean things?" He asked similar questions of the children's teachers and parents, and also compiled data on their school standings, family environment, and reading and television-watching habits. Some 10 years later, when the subjects had reached the age of 19, Eron was able to reexamine about half of the original group. And among the boys, he found a startling relationship between what was seen on television and what Eron termed an aggression rating—a measure of the child's aggressiveness as reported by his classmates. This indicator of violent behavior, Eron reported, depended more on the amount and kinds of violence the boy had seen on television than on any other factor, such as school achievement or economic status.

In all these experiments, the model turned out to have an overriding influence on how well violent behavior was learned. The children were more likely to imitate a model they knew than one who was a stranger, and more likely to imitate one who was in authority than one who was not. A child finds his earliest models in his family. He picks up his first words from his parents, and finds out how to hit, push and kick by doing as his brothers and sisters do. Later the child will learn from other models—his playmates, the adults of his community and the cultural heroes they commonly honor.

The things that children assimilate from all these influences show up in curious ways in their play. Psychologist Franco Ferracuti of Rome University, who specializes in studies of crime, described how children on the island of Sardinia played a version of the game that British and American children know as cops and robbers. The Sardinian child who played the policeman seized one of the group taking the role of robbers

The gentle folk of Malaya

A Semai woman caresses a pet monkey.

Strong evidence that violence and aggression are learned rather than instinctive forms of behavior comes from the Semai of central Malaya. Left to themselves, the 13,000 Semai are so gentle that not a single murder has ever been recorded among them and they do not even feel the need for a police force.

According to anthropologist Robert Dentan, who spent more than a year living with them, the Semai learn to be nonviolent from the time they are children. Youngsters see gentle behavior all around them. Although they hunt and kill animals for food, they also raise large numbers of animals as pets and for trade; the animals they raise they treat tenderly and rarely kill. Adults never hit each other, and if two children appear to be on the verge of a fight,

their parents quickly separate them.

Such pacific behavior may change drastically if the Semai are transplanted to a culture in which they are exposed to violence. In the early 1950s, the British recruited and trained them for a force to fight Communists in Malaya. When some of them were killed in battle by the Communists, their comrades reacted with great ferocity. So aggressive did they become that a veteran later recalled, "We killed, killed, killed. We only thought of killing. Truly we were drunk with blood."

When the fighting was over and the Semai soldiers returned to their homes, they quickly reverted to their old nonviolent ways. At home and abroad, the decisive factor in their behavior was what they were taught.

by the collar, banged his head on the nearest wall and shouted, "Tell me who did it!" The robber child refused to tell, honoring the local tradition of invincible loyalty to members of his own group, and the children standing by kept silent with him. The policeman turned his attention elsewhere for a moment, and the other children helped the robber to make a thrilling escape. The game always ended with victory for the robbers. When American children played cops and robbers in the 1930s, a time when the police enjoyed high public esteem, the young cops generally came out the winners and brought their quarry in successfully—dead or alive.

In the American version, the police served as worthy models that the children unwittingly sought to emulate; for the Sardinian children, the models were those who kept a loyal silence and helped a friend, even one who might be a criminal. But although the models were different, the lesson was the same; the use of violence was justified and, indeed, expected as a part of life.

Violent models are an essential device in military training, which must prepare young people to overcome their reluctance to kill. In some cases outright brutality is demonstrated to shock trainees into acceptance of violence.

One very bloody and effective training technique used by the United States Marine Corps in preparing recruits for combat was known as the "rabbit lesson." An instructor, ostensibly lecturing on jungle survival, held a rabbit in his arms as he talked. The trainees gradually took an interest in the rabbit. Suddenly the instructor whipped out a knife, skinned the creature alive, disemboweled it and hurled its insides at the horrified audience. "That's the last lesson you catch in the U.S. before you leave for Vietnam," recalled one Marine veteran.

Imitation is a lifelong process—people of any age have a tendency to imitate the behavior of others. That such learning continues from childhood into the adult years was shown by elaborate field experiments designed to provide scientific controls in a real-life setting. One such experiment, known as "the brazen bump," was staged at a suburban market by psychologist Mary B. Harris of the University of New Mexico. Her collaborators were students who acted out their aggressive drama in crowded stores. One served as the brazen bumper. Another was the model, who showed one of two reactions. He either feigned anger —"Who do you think you are, just bumping into someone like that? You'd better watch it from now on"—or he politely said, "Excuse me." Then the bumper pushed against one of the shoppers in the store—the unsuspecting subjects of the experiment. Shoppers who had overheard

A Sicilian tradition of violence is reinforced by a mock execution staged by street urchins in Palermo, shortly after the Festival of the Dead. The holiday is marked by gifts to little boys of toy guns, provoking outbursts of mock battles and tableaus like this one.

the model being aggressive themselves tended to be more belligerent to the brazen bumper.

Adults can learn aggression even when the model is repulsive. Perhaps the most egregious example of that phenomenon was noted by Bruno Bettelheim, the eminent psychologist. He recalled that during a year he spent as a prisoner in Nazi concentration camps, he found some of the inmates—especially those who were trusties of the guards—behaved as cruelly to their fellow prisoners as did the guards themselves. They cursed and threatened fellow prisoners, and beat some of them to see who could stand the pain the longest. Some even scrounged the guards' discarded shirts and pants and pieced them together in ragged copies of the guards' uniforms. The guards, brutal as they were, represented a model of success; and so some hapless prisoners reacted by imitating and adopting the behavior of their tormentors. Of course a good deal more than simple imitation was involved; the guards rewarded the trusties for petty treacherous services, and the trusties avoided punishment by doing the bidding of the guards.

The conditioning process of reward and punishment generally reinforces imitation in teaching violence. One of the things that the Bandura experiments showed was that the children were more likely to imitate an aggressive model if he won a skirmish than if he lost—in other words, if he was rewarded—and they did so in spite of budding consciences about right and wrong. One group of children saw a five-minute film in which the aggressive model is rewarded: Rocky takes Johnny's toys and in the final scene plays happily with them while helping himself to bottles of soda and cookies and bouncing on a hobby horse. A second group of children saw a film featuring the same two characters, but in this one Rocky's aggression fails and he is thoroughly thrashed by Johnny. Afterward, the researchers observed and recorded the children's aggressive acts as they played with Bobo and other toys. The children who had seen the aggressor rewarded were far more belligerent in their play. And in postexperiment interviews they made it clear why. The children criticized Rocky as "mean" and "wicked." They knew that his actions were wrong, that is, prohibited by society. Yet they said they would do as he had done all the same. One child commented with unassailable logic, "He got all good toys."

In the most complex of the Bobo doll experiments, Bandura combined the learning mechanisms of reward and imitation—with ominous results. His nursery school subjects were placed in three groups, each of which saw a color film projected on a TV console. Each film showed the aggressive model attacking the Bobo doll while uttering distinct expletives—so that each of the different sequences of violence was verbally identified. In the first film, the aggressor was rewarded handsomely with soda and candy bars. In the second film, the model was punished by means of a spanking. In the third film, the aggressive acts had no apparent consequences.

As previous experiments had indicated, children who saw the model rewarded imitated the film's aggressive acts more than the others did when playing later with Bobo and other toys. But at the end of the experiment the researchers added a new wrinkle. They offered the children rewards such as a glass of fruit juice for every imitative act from the movie they could remember and demonstrate. This incentive quickly established that all the children had learned more aggressive behavior from watching the model than they had displayed without the impetus of a reward. Children thus learn more through observation than they ordinarily show, adding new kinds of aggression to their repertoire and holding them there unseen until a suitable occasion arises—in this case, the promise of a reward for revealing their new knowledge.

Skeptics understandably might ask what hitting a Bobo doll has to do with real-life violence directed at human beings. One answer is that many of the experiments have been successfully repeated using human targets who do not bounce back as resiliently as Bobo. More important, both laboratory findings and evidence from the real world suggest that a kind of generalizing, or carry-over, effect is at work in the learning of aggression. For example, if subjects in experiments are rewarded for one kind of aggression, verbal abuse, they are likely to become more physically aggressive.

They also show the tendency to generalize from one kind of target to another, generalizing from an inanimate Bobo to human targets. This process was demonstrated in the reward experiments of Richard Walters and his colleagues from the University of Waterloo in Canada. They rigged the doll so that every time the child whacked it a mechanism would dispense a small reward—a marble. With this incentive the children enjoyed attacking Bobo, of course, and by the end of the session they had formed the hitting habit. Observed at play afterward, they easily made the switch from Bobo to human targets and proved consistently more aggressive toward their playmates than children who had not been rewarded for pummeling Bobo. (Interestingly, children in these experiments tend to persist in their hitting habit longer when they have been rewarded intermittently—say, a marble every sixth hit—than when the reward arrives every time.)

In all these experiments, children imitated a model because they perceived that the model had been rewarded for his behavior. In a child's own life he learns to repeat what he has done correctly by being rewarded for it, and he learns to avoid what he has done incorrectly by failing to win reward.

R ewards are many and subtle, and in every culture the young child learns early that some of them are to be had for misbehavior—that is, for taking actions that nominally are condemned. Often, aggression is the most effective way—sometimes the only way—of getting what he wants. He gets the toy he wants simply by taking it. He gets his sister to leave him alone by hitting her. As parents have always known intuitively, if he does either and gets away with it, he is likely to do it again; his success is his reward, and a pattern of achieving goals through violence may be established.

If violence brings a reward, it would seem simple enough to prevent that kind of violence by eliminating the reward—every time Johnny snatches Mary's toy, make him give the toy back, consistently enforcing this rule until Johnny learns he cannot get the toy by force. This obvious remedy does not always work, as nearly all parents know. The reason is that the ostensible reward is not always the one actually sought. Johnny may care nothing at all about Mary's toy, and possession of it is not his reward. What Johnny often wants is attention—even if that attention is disapproval—and if he can get this reward only by aggression, he learns to be aggressive. The existence of this mechanism is confirmed by results of an experiment at the University of Illinois nursery school. When teachers there were instructed to ignore aggressive acts—thus denying the aggressor the reward of attention—and to single out cooperative behavior for notice and praise, cooperation increased while belligerence diminished.

Denial of a desired reward is a kind of punishment, and punishment has long been used to influence behavior. It works—but not always in the way it is expected to. Particularly when violent punishment is administered in an attempt to deter violent behavior, it may prove to be counterproductive.

Corporal punishment is traditional in Western cultures. Children are spanked for misbehavior. But the spanking itself can instill a belief in violence. The irony of spanking is illustrated by a magazine cartoon in which a father, with his son over his knee and his hand raised, says, "This will teach you not to hit people." The truth is that the spanking itself is a violent act, and the teacher, in this case the boy's father, is an all-important model, who is getting away with his own violence. If the boy

Egged on by the enthusiastic yells of their classmates, two boys tussle in a schoolyard. The plaudits of their peers are a major factor in inciting young people to fight, while the approval and esteem accorded the winner serve as inducement to further aggression.

wishes to avoid another spanking, he is likely to mend his ways while his father is watching but use the lesson in another fight when his father is not around. In a classic study of aggressive child-rearing practices, Robert Sears of Stanford University and his team interviewed 379 middle-class mothers in the Boston area. They found that both physical punishment and its opposite, extreme permissiveness, were associated with high aggressiveness in their young children. Permissiveness was apparently interpreted by the children as parental approval of their aggressive behavior. By contrast, the least aggressive children came from homes with firm rules that were enforced from the time of infancy in a loving—but nonpunitive—way.

Other investigations of aggression in the family have confirmed and extended these findings among adolescents and younger children, in middle and lower socioeconomic groups, and in urban and rural areas. Aggressive children tended to come from homes where the parents were rejecting and punitive, inconsistent in their guidance and constantly fighting between themselves and undermining each other's values.

Further evidence of the influence on children of punishment by adults comes from studies of cultures like the Eskimos', in which children are never spanked, and grow up to be nonviolent adults. But there is conflicting evidence as well. Another culture long noted for its apparent lack of violence—the English—has also been noted for spanking school children for minor misbehavior. Since as early as 1669, the practice of caning in English schools has survived numerous campaigns to abolish it; it still exists in many schools, and is defended on the grounds that the schoolmasters serve in the place of a parent. Why does it not produce a nation full of openly aggressive Englishmen? There is no satisfactory explanation, and caning in the schools remains an anomaly.

That the caning itself is not responsible for producing good citizens is evident enough. For when corporal punishment was administered to English criminals by the courts, as it was until 1948, it did nothing to chasten the criminals. "I should think the product I am today ought to prove thrashings are no good," wrote one habitual criminal. "After three days it doesn't hurt any more. And the scars soon heal except those on your mind. What you feel is anger, resentment and, most of all, a determination somehow to get your own back. But being deterred? The idea never gets a look-in."

Any punishment, whether corporal or not, may spark further anger and hostility if it is perceived as cruel and arbitrary. Robert Hamblin and his colleagues from Washington University in St. Louis produced this effect in a special class for hyperaggressive boys. Good behavior in the class ordinarily brought the boys tokens that could be redeemed for special privileges, but for purposes of the experiment, tokens the boys had already earned were taken away each time they hit, pushed or fought one another. The loss of the tokens, far from inducing the boys to be docile, so aroused them that the frequency of hitting, pushing and fighting almost doubled.

Rewards and punishments are seldom as obvious as tokens and thrashings. They are woven into the fabric of society so that everything a child sees and hears around him presses him toward—or away from—violence. In America, for instance, violence is considered a desirable characteristic in a boy. To avoid it, particularly in self-defense, is a mark against him; if he consistently acts nonviolently, he loses status. Practically all American fathers encourage their children to "stand up for your rights." Interviews in six different countries—the Philippines, Mexico, the United States, India, Okinawa and Kenya—indicate also that mothers in the United States are more likely to encourage fighting in self-defense than mothers anywhere else—they gave praise for aggression in upholding the family name and in many other similar situations. This finding was buttressed by the Sears survey of Boston mothers, which showed that more than 80 per cent of them told their children to fight back if picked on. And one authority reported to a committee investigating violence that when one Chicago mother was called into school by a teacher because her son was always getting into fights, her first question was, "Does he win?"

Even more powerful motivation for aggression may be provided by the attitudes of a youngster's peers. Youthful urban gangs furnish dramatic examples of this influence. In San Francisco one gang had bizarre entrance requirements: an aspirant won 10 points for each unprovoked assault on a stranger and he had to accumulate 100 points to be granted full-fledged membership. Gangs have been known to keep scrapbooks detailing their exploits. In New York the district attorney's office attempted to suppress newspaper publicity about street gangs on the grounds that it served to provide an incentive for further violence.

Just a few words of praise may be sufficient incentive for children and adults to act aggressively. How few has been demonstrated in laboratory experiments with the so-called "aggression machine," a harmlessly diabolical gadget that measures how much punishment a subject is willing to administer to a victim. Typically, the subject is seated at an elaborate control panel and led to believe that the buttons on the panel will deliver an electric shock to another person as part of a learning experiment. The "victim" is actually a confederate of the ex-

continued on page 60

The Wren and the Bear

A war between creatures that walk and those that fly ends righteously in the rout of the aggressors, the ground dwellers. One of them, the bear, had triggered the battle by invading a wren's nest.

The grim world of the Grimms

Long before television or movies came into being, children were exposed to violence in one of the oldest and most beguiling forms of juvenile entertainment—fairy tales. To most people the stories are harmless entertainment, but some authorities believe they influence children toward violent behavior.

The stories exist in similar forms in many cultures, but the most famous and perhaps the most violently aggressive are the tales that were recorded in the early 1800s by the German brothers, Jacob and Wilhelm Grimm. An immediate success, Grimms' *Fairy Tales* continue to be the most widely read book in Germany after the Bible, and millions of copies have been sold in 70 languages.

The world depicted by the brothers Grimm and illustrated here in Arthur Rackham's drawings for a 1909 edition, includes child-eating witches, poisoned apples and evil giants. Experts are divided about the tales' impact. Some, notably psychologist Bruno Bettelheim, hold that the tales prepare children for reality by confronting them with real problems, such as fear and death. They also believe that the tales promote morality by making a virtuous hero an attractive figure. Other psychologists, however, feel the tales are needlessly cruel and teach that violence is a proper response to bad behavior.

Little Red Riding Hood

The heroine of the Grimms' best-known fairy tale
greets the wolf, who is disguised as her grandmother.
The wolf proceeds to eat her, but all works out
well when she is rescued from his belly by a huntsman.

The Valiant Little Tailor

Two evil giants uproot huge trees and beat each other
to death, after having been tricked into a fight by a
tailor who was offered a reward for destroying them.

Hänsel and Gretel

Imprisoned by a nearsighted witch, who is fattening
him for a meal, Hänsel fools his captor by offering
her a scrawny knucklebone and deceiving her
into thinking that he is much too thin to be eaten.

Sweetheart Roland

A wicked witch tears herself to death in a bramble bush, trapped there by Roland, protective sweetheart of the stepdaughter she has been chasing after.

perimeter and no shock is delivered. With no more encouragement from the experimenter than two words—"That's good"—college students are willing to deliver more "shocks" of higher intensity than if they receive no praise.

How such attitudes can influence behavior was demonstrated by David Mantell, an American-born clinical psychologist on the staff of the Max Planck Institute in Munich. Mantell addressed himself to a study of the way family atmosphere influenced some young Americans to volunteer for service in the Vietnam War but influenced others to refuse to serve. He interviewed 25 members of the United States Army Special Forces—the Green Berets—and contrasted them with 25 men who had resisted the draft. The two groups came from homes that were stable, but that, by their own accounts, differed markedly in parental models, in rewards and punishments, and in values and atmosphere.

More than half of the Green Berets' fathers had themselves been war veterans. They provided military models for their sons from an early age, for many of those fathers had brought home proud trophies of combat, told war stories and required marching, saluting and other forms of military drill at home—practices that over the years served to condition their sons to obedience and military activity. Just as many of the resisters' fathers had served in the armed forces, but they made different kinds of models and provided different kinds of conditioning: they had no trophies, no stories, no drills.

And that was not all. Almost to a man, the Green Berets had had cold, tyrannical fathers who had dealt out severe punishment in the form of beating with belts, boards or chains. The resisters described affectionate fathers; few could recall any physical punishment, and their good behavior had been reinforced with praise. "Violence does not emerge in a vacuum," Mantell concluded, sounding a variation on Bandura's theme. "It is planted by example, and continually reinforced or extinguished by experience."

While direct personal experiences—with family, friends and school—are crucial in conditioning behavior, less direct influences have become increasingly important, particularly in the industralized nations. Much of what people learn now reaches them through the communications media. Books and pictures have long affected beliefs and actions, but two 20th Century developments—movies and television—have proved uniquely efficient in disseminating ideas and, it seems, in inculcating aggressiveness.

The two media are similar in that they simulate a realistic world in which the viewer can feel he belongs, but television apparently has a far more pervasive effect on young minds. The reasons are not hard to find. Because programs come from far and wide, television may act as a cross-cultural influence, cutting across national idiosyncrasies and serving to give people of varied values and heritages common information. Because it comes right into the home, it has the immediacy, if not the intimacy, of a family member. As such, it serves as model, rewarder and conditioner all in one. And unlike the printed word, which requires reading skills, television's vivid images and spoken words demand only a child's attention.

But perhaps the major reason children (and adults) are so influenced by television is that they are exposed to so much of it. Hour after hour, day after day, its messages are hammered into the mind. In the United States, some 97 per cent of all homes have at least one set, and it is turned on a mind-boggling average of six hours and 11 minutes daily. Some American youngsters spend more time watching television (up to 49 hours a week) than they do in school. But the United States is not alone in its absorption with television; the phenomenon is worldwide. The Japanese outwatch Americans; 70 per cent of Japanese sets are turned on by 8 a.m., and they continue for an astonishing seven hours and 17 minutes a day.

The great amount of time people spend watching television implies an enormous impact for its messages. And in most countries the messages preach violence, displaying it and glorifying it. There is so much on the air in the United States that George Gerbner, dean of The Annenberg School of Communications at the University of Pennsylvania, devised a "violence profile" to measure it. Analysts monitored 33 hours of entertainment programs broadcast nationwide in a sample week, noting each specific act of violence shown. This information was used in compiling an annual index of TV violence. In 1973, at least some violence was contained in 70 per cent of the programs. Children's cartoons averaged eight episodes of violence an hour. A newspaper cartoon summed up the attitude of many American parents: "We moved out of the city so he wouldn't be exposed to all that crime, sex and violence," says the cartoon mother smugly—while in the background her son is immersed in a violent television show. It has been estimated that by the age of 18 or so the average American youngster will have viewed more than 18,000 murders on television.

British television presents almost as much violence. And in Germany, Heribert Heinrichs of the University of Hildesheim earned himself the sobriquet of corpse counter for his meticulous tabulation of tele-

A bamboo cane at the ready reminds Calcutta school children of the painful penalty for misbehavior. Its use is not effective, most child behavior experts agree; in the words of one expert, corporal punishment merely teaches the child "that he lives in a violent world, that it is better . . . to be the spanker than the spankee." Nonetheless, caning is still a common practice in many schools around the world, including those in England and the United States.

vision violence. In a single week he counted 103 deaths, 52 brawls, 27 shoot-outs, eight robberies and a plethora of other violence in the form of arson, rape and torture depicted on the German screen. Among the high points of his collection were episodes in which a boy threatened his mother with a bread knife and a group of men attempted to pollute the drinking water of a whole community. His figures did not come from news or from sober documentaries; all were derived from sensational drama shows that in Heinrichs' opinion were aimed at touching a special nerve in the viewers.

In television-addicted Japan, not an evening goes by without two or three hours of bloody samurai or *yakuza* (gangster) shows. There are even specialized craftsmen, called *tateshi,* who spend their days dreaming up complex, shocking or exotic sequences of violence for the camera. The prize effort of one highly esteemed *tateshi* was a series that was built around a middle-aged samurai who was quiet and unassuming but who achieved great popularity with viewers because of his unique method of murder: in every one of the installments he killed at least one villain by disemboweling him.

But not all television violence is dramatic make-believe; a good deal of it is real violence in the form of news. In France, Pierre Debuche, director of a weekly called *Loisirs Jeunes (Young Leisure),* sees more harm to children in what he calls the gratuitous violence shown on the news than he does in fictional violence. The only good thing to be said for the news, in his opinion, is that it is a program children watch evenings in the company of their parents. "They are not alone in front of the screen as they would be in the afternoon," he points out, "and violence, like any other bad thing, is taken very differently by a child if he is in the reassuring world of his family."

Psychologists Guy Cumberbatch and Dennis Howitt of Britain take a similar view. They hold that critics of television violence should worry more about the 9 o'clock news than they do about the violent cartoon comedies young children like so much. While in theory the contents of the cartoons make them among the most violent programs on television, they feel the violence is offset by the humor.

Some defenders of television have cited the catharsis notions of Aristotle and Freud, suggesting that television violence provides a healthy outlet for children's aggressive tendencies *(Chapter 5).* In Japan—a land of great swings between aggressive and pacific behavior *(pages 20-21)*—one producer asserted: "Violence is like salt to our cuisine." But such defenders are in the minority. All over the world, psychologists, critics of the arts, state leaders—and recently, people in the television industry itself—have become concerned about the high percentage of violence shown on television screens everywhere.

One result of this concern was a three-year study sponsored by the United States government, which, beginning in 1969, commissioned 23 projects on the effects of television violence. The projects involved 7,500 youngsters from the age of three to 19 who came from all sorts of socio-economic backgrounds—black and white, urban and rural, middle-class and poor families.

One of these experiments tested the findings of the Bobo doll studies by using regular television programing instead of laboratory films. Young children were shown a three-and-a-half-minute segment of a violent show that included two fistfights, two shootings and a knifing. A control group was shown a TV sports event. Then the children were led individually to a kind of aggression machine. One button on the control panel, they were told, would help a child playing a special game in the next room. The other would hurt him.

Not only were the children who saw the violent TV show more likely to push the "hurt button," but another experiment enabled researchers also to predict, to some extent, which children would be the more aggressive. The children were photographed while they watched so that the researchers could study their emotional reactions to highlights of the program. The boys (though not the girls) who showed pleasure or happiness during the violent action sequences proved to be more inclined to push the hurt button.

A second type of study, conducted independently of the government program by F. B. Steuer and a team at the University of North Carolina, pursued the effects of TV violence outside the laboratory, in a natural setting. Children at a nursery school were first observed in 10 play sessions and rated for their aggressive behavior—hitting, kicking, choking or throwing objects at someone. The children previously had been matched in pairs according to the amount of television they ordinarily watched. Now one member from each pair was shown, on 11 different days, an aggressive TV show taken from among those ordinarily broadcast on Saturday mornings. The other member of the pair saw a nonaggressive show on each of these days. Afterward, the children were observed during natural play. In every matched pair of children, the child who had viewed the violent show had become more aggressive than his partner. A similar experiment in Belgium had similar results. At a private institution for delinquent boys, an international team of scientists found that violent commercial movies increased aggressive be-

Child's play with a grisly twist

Violent toys make children behave more aggressively, according to a study at the University of Indiana, and a macabre escalation of make-believe brutality in the 1970s—particularly in the United States—troubled behavioral scientists as well as parents. Stores sold dolls that could be caged, sawed in half or beaten. So extreme was one toy—the swinging blade at right—that protests forced a halt in its sale.

Violent toys were not an American monopoly, of course. But the American toy makers gave the violence a new twist, and in their zeal presented even such a traditionally French contrivance as the guillotine as a plaything.

Modeled after the guillotine, this gadget swings a blade that threatens to slice the victim in half. Parents demanded —and won—its removal from the market.

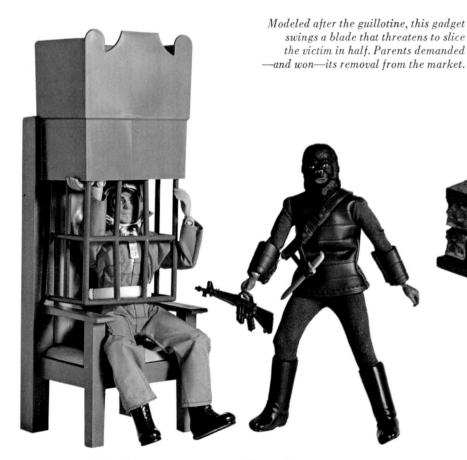

Derived from a monster movie, Planet of the Apes, this set includes a well-armed gorilla and a victim who is trapped by a cage that lowers around him.

This vicious trio, labeled "Professional Agents/Crime Killers," includes one man armed with a bull whip, another with a steel hook and one with bow and arrow.

A pair of high-kicking karate dolls can be activated by a child so they will chop and kick violently for what the box describes as "authentic karate action."

havior—despite the presence of counselors who ordinarily keep a lid on fights and arguments.

Beyond the overwhelming evidence that watching television seems to incite the urge to emulate it, there appear to be other effects that are just as alarming. Youngsters permitted a heavy diet of television violence may become emotionally immune to acts of violence by others. Victor Cline of the University of Utah wired boys aged five to 12 with instruments that measured their pulses, perspiration and other physiological effects that accompany emotional arousal. He then showed them a violent sequence from the boxing movie *The Champion*. Cline found that those subjects who watched television 25 hours a week or more showed significantly less emotional arousal than those who watched infrequently. He concluded that extensive previous exposure to television had so conditioned them to violence that it may have robbed them of normal sympathy for the victim.

Television conditioning can so accustom heavy viewers to violence that they acquire vastly distorted notions of how much violence actually occurs in their own neighborhoods. In a telephone survey conducted by the University of Pennsylvania, a sampling of households in four U.S. metropolitan areas was asked: "During any given week, what are your chances of being involved in some type of violence? About fifty-fifty, or one in one hundred?" People who watched more than four hours of television a day tended to answer 50-50; those who watched less than two hours a day answered one in 100. By police statistics the correct answer was only one in 100—the answer given by people whose television viewing was low. Persons whose TV viewing is high, in other words, expect to find more violence in the world around them than there actually is.

Such evidence persuaded government authorities in many nations to exercise greater control over the violence that television brought before young eyes. Generally, the more violent programs are kept off the air during daytime and early evening hours. In the United States, most broadcasters agreed to a voluntary code for keeping unsuitable shows from children—they are not broadcast until after a time when youngsters are assumed to be sleeping. And some effort was made to eliminate the indiscriminate punching and beating that—although presented humorously—was endemic in programs prepared for the very young.

Even news shows are, in some places, edited with regard for their effect on young viewers. British television producers kept the more violent sequences of the daily news out of the bulletins shown before 9 p.m. The Japanese went further; they established a five-minute news program at 6 p.m. tailored just for children. *The Children's News*—which dates back to 1959—deliberately screened out scenes of violence. In 1967, when there were riotous demonstrations by radicals in Japan, *The Children's News* showed none of them. "The judgment of the children is not mature enough to understand the violence," said Seinosuke Miwa, the producer. How much effect stringent regulation of television can have remains to be seen. For no single influence seems to make a culture violent or nonviolent. There is evidence that the Japanese, who watch violent television more than Americans do, are generally less aggressive than Americans. The multitude of elements that together make up a culture must all play a part in teaching people to act violently or peaceably.

Some of these elements have now been recognized. The models and rewards presented by parents and communications media seem to be universal, present in all cultures in different forms and with different aims. Other pressures seem unique to certain societies. The American disposition toward violence, for example, has been blamed on a number of factors. The heritage of the frontier, where violence was often necessary for survival, creates traditions honoring violence. The ready availability of firearms puts deadly weapons at hand, increasing the likelihood of their use and somehow instilling the notion that they ought to be used. Even the vaunted ideal of equality of opportunity may, in the opinion of some experts, set the stage for violence. American laws and tradition maintain that any poor child can grow up to be President, or rich and successful, or at least comfortably middle class, and the possibility has subtly been altered into a requirement: every child should. Many do, of course, but many others see the goal eluding them and, in their frustration, turn to action that their society has taught them can solve a problem: violence.

The rise of the shoot-'em-up

The opening blast of a medium extolling violence was signaled December 21, 1903, by the pistol firing that opened the premiere screening of The Great Train Robbery, the first full-fledged Western moving picture. The shot bore no relationship to the plot of the film; the director, Edwin S. Porter, deliberately exploited the sensational attraction of violence to catch the audience's attention.

From the moment back in 1903 when the villain fired his gun from the screen in *The Great Train Robbery (left)*, violence has been an indispensable part of the Wild West motion picture. This enduringly popular art form is not only a reflection of the human fascination with violence but is apparently also a promoter of violence. Laboratory experiments have shown that children become more aggressive physically and verbally after they have been exposed to violence in Westerns and other films.

In their dual role as mirror and instigator of violence, Westerns have taken on a grisly new dimension as the years have passed. In the old days, the violence consisted mainly of fist fights and barroom brawls, portrayed so artificially they could not be taken as serious models for the viewer's behavior; the violence was make-believe, not real. Western heroes were good guys who inevitably triumphed over the villains. Violence was mainly the province of the bad guys; heroes resorted to it only to uphold law and order.

But over the years the violence has become not only realistic but also indiscriminate and unjustifiable. Heroes and villains are caught up in orgies of shootings and beatings that are displayed in bloody, even loving, detail, and there is no longer any effort to justify the mayhem.

This grim evolution has occurred in clearly delineated stages. The charade-like violence typical of the silent films acquired impact with the addition of sound. World War II added stark new realism, and in the years that followed, the violence escalated rapidly until it became the films' major preoccupation.

The silents' stylized charade

The first Westerns were silent and short films—lasting only about 12 minutes—shot in the wilds of industrialized New Jersey. They were filled with action but included little believable violence. Partly because of the lack of sound, they resembled pantomime illusions, and even if a killing was included—a rare occurrence—it was artificial and unconvincing.

The focus of the silents was the hero, a romantic figure who always won out, usually with his fists but occasionally—and reluctantly—with a gun. And always the script gave a powerful reason why he had to use violence in his commendable crusade against evil.

A grimacing Ken Maynard tosses a villain in the air in Somewhere in Sonora, the story of a man trying to rescue a boy from a life of banditry. Maynard, portraying a mild-mannered man, resorted to violence only to save a friend.

Released from jail, cowboy hero Hoot Gibson singlehandedly knocks out three bad guys who have caused his arrest on false charges in a film titled Action. The he-man Gibson rarely carried a weapon in his pictures; when the script did call for him to use a gun, he borrowed one and stuck it into his boot.

In Broncho Twister, hero Tom Mix draws a gun to rescue an abducted lady. Gunplay was unusual for Mix, who generally subdued victims with his fists, or a lasso. When forced to shoot, he aimed not to kill, but to injure, his target.

Lively but bloodless brawling

The advent of sound in the late 1920s accentuated the violence in Westerns, while at the same time, the amount of violence began to increase and more attention was paid to its staging. Such changes were most evident in carefully produced, costly films such as *They Died with Their Boots On (above)*, but it was also apparent in the so-called B Westerns—mass-produced horse operas with low budgets. Still there was an air of unreality. Men were beaten, shot and killed without a murmur of pain or a drop of blood showing.

Errol Flynn, playing the role of General Custer, hurls a tomahawk-wielding Indian over his shoulder in one of the biggest Westerns of the 1940s, They Died with Their Boots On. It featured a mass but bloodless slaughter. After this scene, Custer himself died, falling, one critic said, "with the grace of a dancer."

A stunt man leaps from a galloping horse to capture the villain of a B movie called Lone Star Trail. Acrobatic stunt men contributed greatly to the elaborately staged violence of the B movies.

An invincible Western hero, Buck Jones holds some villains at bay after shooting three in Arizona Bound. Jones and his horse had just come crashing through the window of the saloon in a miraculous feat that left both completely unscathed.

A savage fight erupts between father (John Wayne) and stepson (Montgomery Clift) in Red River. Only after the War, when characters were treated as realistic individuals rather than stereotypes, did movies showing violence between members of a family become acceptable.

A brutal beating is endured by Alan Ladd in Shane as he is kneed in the groin by villainous cowboys. This classic motion picture made the hero as upright as any traditional good guy but as ready to engage in violence as the bad guys.

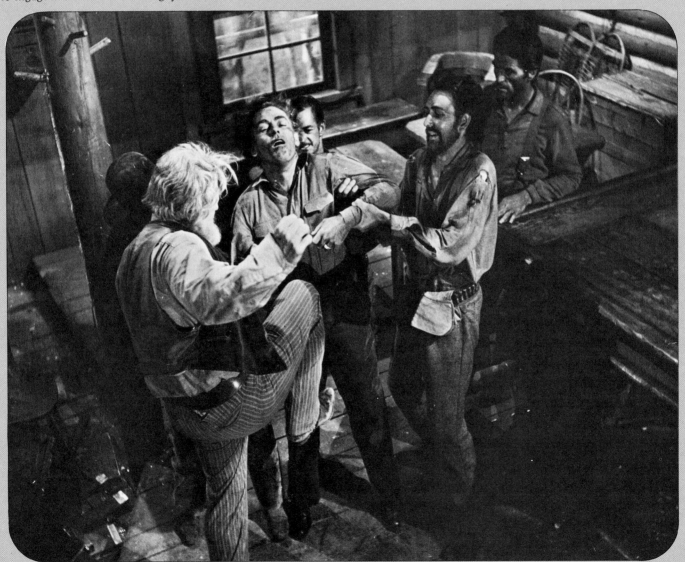

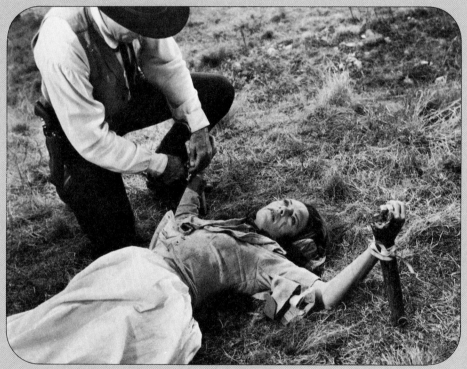

In Five Bold Women, Jeff Morrow bends
over the body of a murderer ambushed
and then tortured by Indians while
she was being escorted to prison.
In the new realism of the Western even
women were acknowledged to be both
perpetrators of violence and victims of it.

Brutality and gore
of the new realism

After World War II, violence in the
Western took a grimly serious turn.
Unpleasantness and suffering were no
longer glossed over. Vicious fist fights
produced bloody faces, and victims died
painful deaths. At the same time, sets,
costumes and stories became more realistic. Characters were less stereo-
typed: the hero was no longer always
the good guy, and good guys were just
as vulnerable to violence as villains.

But perhaps the surest indicator was
the change in the attitude toward wom-
en. Female characters had been notable
for their absence from the Western;
when included they had been treated
with storybook chivalry. Now the ar-
tificiality was dropped. Women struck
and shot men—and in turn were beat-
en, tortured and killed.

As Will Penny in the picture of that name, Charlton Heston is brutally stabbed with a knife by Donald Pleasence and two accomplices. Heston played a scruffy drifter, while Pleasence was a sadistic religious fanatic—roles seldom found in the traditional Western.

Choking almost to the point of death, Clint Eastwood is dragged through town at the end of a rope in Hang 'Em High. The film featured beatings and hangings, and TIME reported that in some scenes "the necrophilic camera lingers lovingly over the dead and dying."

An obsession with savagery

Ironically, it took a series of films produced in Italy—the so-called spaghetti Westerns—to inspire movie makers to the highest level of violence. The Italian films—which first appeared in the 1960s—characteristically included the slaughter of great numbers of people, and close-ups of bullet wounds, gushing blood and battered bodies. By now the violence was cynical and totally indiscriminate. Villains got away with torturing and killing innocent people, and the hero who resorted to violence only to uphold law and order was a relic of the past.

The Italian films were accepted so eagerly by the public that Hollywood quickly began to imitate and outdo them. Nothing at all was left to the imagination of the viewer as the Western—which formerly had been an innocent form of escapist entertainment—wallowed in orgies of violence.

"The bloodiest battle ever put on film,"
one critic wrote of the final shoot-out in
The Wild Bunch. An intentionally brutal
story about a group of aging, stupid and
morally bankrupt outlaws attempting one
last big robbery, the film came to its
climax with the massacre of all but one
of the band. The producer, Sam
Peckinpah, said of the public response to
the violence in The Wild Bunch, "I
rubbed their noses in it . . . they loved it."

Coming to Blows

"Everything went wrong that day," explained the motorist, a 26-year-old British shipping clerk. "I had a row with one of the other clerks about an invoice or something and then after work I found I'd been given a £2 ticket for parking my car to cause obstruction. One thing and another, the rush hour got on my nerves. Then, when I was almost home, following slowly behind a line of traffic, the car in front stopped and the chap decided to park there with a whole lot of cars behind him. I was furious and tooted him, but he waved me on. People behind were also tooting, but he started walking away, so I drove my car right into the back of his. Luckily, there was no one inside his car because the boot and rear bumper were badly dented."

The tale told by the clerk—whose words are excerpted from a case study in *Aggression on the Road* by British psychologist M. H. Parry —indicates some important factors that are at work when people commit acts of violence and aggression. The clerk had been aroused to an emotional state of anger by a series of frustrating events during the course of the day: the row with his fellow worker, the parking ticket and the jammed rush-hour traffic. Then came the last straw: the man ahead stopped his car, got out and walked away from it, and that triggered the clerk, pushing him over the line from a state of anger to an act of aggression. The actual commission of that act was made possible by the fact that he had a weapon at hand, his own automobile, and a target was readily available in the form of the car parked directly in front of him in the middle of the street.

These four ingredients—arousal, trigger, weapon and target—are generally present in most acts of human aggression. It is not very surprising that psychologists do not agree as to the relative importance of each. Like most psychological mechanisms, those that are associated with aggression frequently overlap, and they may take changing and elusive forms. Furthermore, individual actions may vary widely, depending upon the potential aggressor's previous experience and learning. But in almost every case the four elements are present, and —with the important exceptions of cold-blooded, unemotional acts, such as those committed by psychopaths or hired killers—no one can behave aggressively until he has been aroused.

Arousal involves both the mind and the body. It has physical effects: the heart beats faster and the breathing accelerates; the face may flush; the hands may shake or become clammy with perspiration. The symptoms are involuntary, part of the physiological reaction to stress that gets the body ready for some kind of action —the precise form of which is yet to be determined. Such arousal may be an indication not only of anger but also of fear, joy, sexual desire or physical activity—almost anything that alerts the body to be prepared for special effort. Arousal to anger seems to come about principally when the individual perceives pain, frustration or aggression against himself. These experiences seem to stimulate an individual directly toward acting aggressively. But an unusual series of experiments indicates that any kind of arousal may be expressed in aggression. All that is necessary is the arousal; how the aroused individual behaves depends fundamentally on what he thinks he should do.

The evidence for this thesis was obtained by psychologists Stanley Schachter and Jerome E. Singer at the University of Minnesota. Schachter and Singer injected a number of subjects with epinephrine, a stimulant that produces heart pounding and other symptoms of emotional arousal. They gave another group of subjects a sham injection that would produce no effects whatsoever. In each group, some of the subjects were informed that they would experience some physiological arousal; others were not. Each subject was then placed in a room with someone who was presented as a fellow guinea pig but was actually a confederate of the experimenters'. The confederate's task was to feign an emotion—in some cases euphoria, in others anger—and to see what the subject of the experiment would do. When the confederate was being euphoric, he jumped around the room, flying paper airplanes and playing basketball with crumpled-up paper. When he was being angry, he cursed and ripped up copies of a questionnaire that the subjects had been given to fill out.

Afterward the subjects were asked to describe how they had felt while under the influence of the shot they had been given. To a certain extent, all the subjects, regardless of which shot they had been given, were influenced by the performance of the confederate, as might be expected from the normal tendency to follow the leader no matter what the circumstances. But the subjects most profoundly influenced by the confederate were the ones who had received the shot of epinephrine and had *not* been told what they were to expect. Those subjects interpreted their heart-pounding as happiness if they had seen the confederate behaving euphorically, and believed themselves to be angry if they had seen him behaving angrily. There was more than willy-nilly imitation involved. With hearts pounding and faces flushed, they knew they felt something, but they were vague and uncertain about what it was, and so they drew on the performance of their companion to make sense out of an otherwise confusing situation.

Psychologists Schachter and Singer concluded from the experiment that anger, fear, joy, hope and sex, far from being discrete and specialized emotions, may all arise from the same general state of arousal, which any excitement can produce. Whether an individual in this state will commit an act of aggression, and what form his aggression will take, thus would depend upon his previous learning and experience.

The way that arousal unconnected with aggression may stimulate aggression was tested even more directly by psychologist Dolf Zillmann in experiments he conducted at the University of Pennsylvania. He used motion pictures of various kinds—not just violent ones, which are known to incite violent behavior—to arouse his subjects, then gauged their aggressiveness.

Zillmann had his experimenters administer electric shocks to three groups of male students. Then he showed the students three different movies: one a tame educational film about Marco Polo's travels; another a violent prizefighting scene, and the third an erotic film. Finally, he gave the subjects a chance to retaliate against the same experimenters who had previously tormented them. He discovered that those students who had seen the erotic film were most willing to deliver the shock to the experimenters.

Zillmann's finding that an erotic arousal can easily be converted into an aggressive response may help explain the fact that an unusually high percentage of murders are precipitated by quarrels between lovers. In the United States more women die violently in the bedroom than anywhere else. A psychoanalyst who interviewed 75 persons who killed their spouses in England, France, Germany, the United States and Greece found that the couples had previously had strong sexual ties. It may be that lovers sustain so heightened a state of arousal that in even a small misunderstanding, sexual excitement is easily switched into anger—which in turn results in violence.

The explanation for this may be biological. Physiologists know from

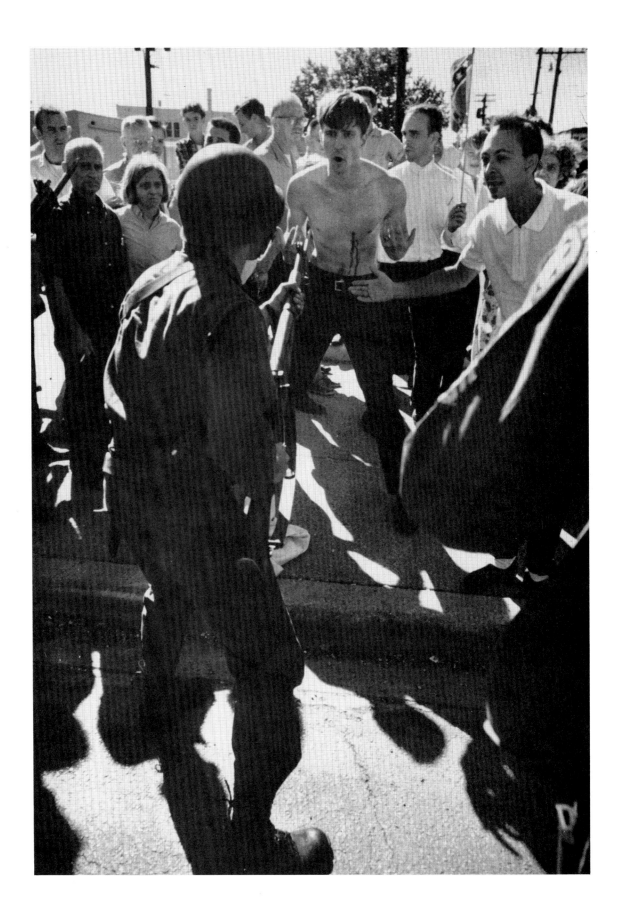

experiments conducted on animals that the centers in the brain that appear to mediate sex and aggression are clustered so closely together that electric stimulation of one part of a male monkey's brain will cause him to have a penile erection, while stimulation of another area only a millimeter away will produce extreme rage. This leads to the conclusion that sexual arousal and aggression in humans may be so closely related that even the smallest misunderstanding between lovers can easily explode into violence.

While experiments indicate that any kind of emotional arousal can lead to violence, some kinds appear to be more likely to do so. One is pain. A person who strikes his finger with a hammer may react by kicking the wall or punching the table. Laboratory experiments by psychologist Nathan Azrin have demonstrated that animals also respond violently to pain. Azrin inflicted pain on rats, monkeys, snakes and opossums. When he shocked two rats in the same cage, they instantly reared up on their hind legs, bared their teeth, swatted each other with their forepaws and bit savagely—much as a human suffering a headache might snap angrily at a companion who has nothing to do with his headache.

Other animals tested by Azrin reacted in their own way. When the monkeys were shocked, they lashed out with their paws. Opossums hissed, while the snakes hissed and encircled the objects of their aggression. And all of these species attempted to bite other animals—live or stuffed—that were placed in the cages with them.

Pain does not have to be so acute as a hammer blow or an electric shock in order to arouse a human being. The same effect may be achieved by petty annoyances and discomforts, such as sounds (dripping faucets and incessant knocking) and bad weather, which makes most people irritable. In the summer of 1967, when 17 cities in the United States were torn by riots, investigators discovered a surprising fact: the weather had followed a similar pattern in all of them, and presumably it had a significant effect on what happened. It had been pleasant enough until just a day before the rioting broke out. Then the temperature shot up sharply; and in those cities where the heat was the most severe and persistent, the riots lasted the longest. Obviously, the root causes of the rioting ran much deeper than the weather; they had to do with social frustrations and a great many other factors. But the sudden and oppressive heat contributed to the rioters' state of arousal. It made people physically uncomfortable, frayed their tempers and drove them from stifling apartments to look for relief outdoors in the streets. There, in the company of great numbers of other people

A bloodied teen-age youth and a soldier square off at a civil rights demonstration near Chicago in 1966, after inciting each other to aggression. The boy taunted the soldier, who responded by gashing the youth with his bayonet. Aroused by the pain, the boy screamed back, "Go ahead, stab me again, you white nigger!"

similarly aroused, they were easily provoked into acting aggressively.

If pain serves as an effective emotional arouser, so too does the threat of pain. Obviously, anyone who is struck by another person feels the desire to strike back (whether or not he does so). But overt aggression is not necessary for arousal: a mere threat of aggression is sufficient to arouse its target, and the threat does not have to be spoken. Some intriguing insights into human behavior come from the studies of the effects, on animals and people, of threats conveyed by the eyes and body. In these investigations, the stare or body movement was perceived as an aggressive act, and the animal or person toward whom it was directed was immediately aroused.

Scientists who study animal behavior know that the dominant monkey of a group will ward off a rival with a stare, and that a stare will arouse a monkey even if a human being does the staring. When one

psychologist directed a merciless gaze at monkeys in his laboratory, the animals responded by staring back, then baring their teeth, beating on the ground and screeching loudly—all signs of an imminent attack. (For this reason, zookeepers are warned not to stare at monkeys when feeding them and tending their cages.)

The stare has unsettling effects on human behavior, too. In many cultures some of the gods are said to be possessed of an evil eye, with which they bring terrible violence to unlucky or misbehaving humans. And in other parts of the world barroom brawls and schoolyard fights in countless numbers have started with a stare and the question, "What are you looking at?"

The power of the stare to arouse deep-seated feelings in human beings was demonstrated by psychologist Phoebe Ellsworth and her colleagues at Stanford University in 1972. Ellsworth's experiments had the opposite effect of the monkey's aggressive responses, however, for instead of staring back or attacking, the subjects chose to flee. Ellsworth set up a series of experiments at a site familiar to practically everyone, a traffic intersection in a suburban area. An experimenter, riding a dilapidated motor scooter, stopped at a red traffic signal alongside the car of an unsuspecting driver. From a distance of four or five feet, the investigator fixed the driver with an unswerving stare and maintained it until the traffic light turned green, while a collaborator posted nearby noted the effects and timed them with a stop watch.

The results were startling and consistent. A second or two after a driver realized he was being stared at, he averted his own eyes and began to fidget. He glanced frequently at the red traffic light, then fumbled with his clothing or the car radio and raced the engine. An occasional driver glanced furtively back at the staring investigator, only to avert his gaze again as soon as their eyes met. When at last the light turned green, the driver sped away. By the collaborators' stop watches, drivers who had been stared at traveled across the intersection almost one and a half seconds faster than drivers crossing the same intersection who had not been stared at.

To make certain that the drivers did not mistake the stare for a challenge to a race, the psychologists repeated the experiment in two variations. In one, the experimenters appeared in the role of pedestrians instead of scooter riders, and stared at drivers from a position on the sidewalk. In another they stared at fellow pedestrians. Either way, the hapless persons who had been stared at fled across the intersection with all possible speed. Ellsworth and her colleagues concluded that "a stare is generally perceived as a signal of hostile intent," a threat. Un-

Barely able to control his emotions, an enraged young Czech thrusts himself into the path of stoic Soviet soldiers, part of the force invading Prague in 1968, and angrily demands that they turn back. So aroused were the Czechs by the threat to their homeland that, though they could not hope to repel the Russian Army, resistance flared across the country; tanks were blown up and a train derailed.

able or unwilling to meet the threat with a counterattack, the drivers and the pedestrians her colleagues stared at chose to flee.

Many people see crowding as another serious threat. Anthropologist Edward T. Hall believes that individuals have a deep-rooted need for a kind of psychological elbow room, and that they are aroused by invasions of personal space. He found subtle proof of his theory when he broached it to his Harvard colleague Roger Brown. On first hearing it Brown was skeptical; as the two men talked, Hall imperceptibly edged his chair nearer to Brown, who reacted quite unconsciously, not noticing until Hall pointed out that in the course of only a few moments' conversation, Brown had moved his chair several feet backward away from Hall. Without even being aware of it, Brown was guarding his personal space; he was fleeing from a deeply sensed but inarticulate threat to his psychological elbow room.

That threats or pain would arouse aggressive emotions seems almost obvious. But another kind of arousal does not have such an obvious connection with aggression: frustration. So elusive and complex is frustration that psychologists were a long time in recognizing its importance in aggression, and they still do not agree with one another on the mechanisms by which it works.

As defined by psychologists, frustration is the emotion generated by interference with a person's progress toward a goal. Such a definition explains the aggressive reaction of the British motorist, who was frustrated in his desire to get home through an impossible traffic jam. It also explains countless other outbursts that occur on a larger scale. The suburban railways of Rio de Janeiro, for instance, daily carry some 500,000 commuters who have a special incentive for getting to work on time. Unemployment in Brazil runs so high that lines form at every factory gate well before opening time, 7 a.m., and anyone not on hand to report for work runs the risk of losing a day's pay, and maybe a full-time job, to someone who is standing in line. But the Brazilian trains are so antiquated, overcrowded, inefficiently run and prone to breakdown that almost daily the commuters who use them are hard put to get to work —and some of those who do get there spend six hours a day making the round trip.

Brazilians bore this mounting frustration more or less peaceably until one morning during the summer of 1975, when a train pulled into a certain station an hour late, already packed, and 4,000 commuters stood on the station platform waiting to board. In the circumstances—with a crowd already primed by a history of previous frustrations and aroused to anger by that morning's delay—the arrival of the jammed train was too much. The crowd exploded, wrecked that train and stoned the next two trains that went by on another track, destroying the very transportation on which they depended so heavily to get to, and keep, their jobs.

Psychologists have been studying frustration for years, setting up experiments, egging people on and then deliberately blocking them short of their goals in order to gain a better understanding of human reactions. Young school children were enticed with toys and then were forbidden to play with them. Not surprisingly, the children reacted by fighting among themselves.

In one rather diabolical experiment, 10-year-old children were assigned the task of building columns out of bottle stoppers with the promise of a prize for completing the job. Each was told that under his table was an electric button, which when pressed would jiggle the table next to him and make his neighbor's pile of stoppers come tumbling down. He was also told that if his own table shook, it did so because somebody else had caused it to shake.

As each child worked at making a pile of stoppers, the experimenter, not a neighboring child, caused the table to shake from time to time, sometimes only making the stoppers tremble, other times making them tumble down. When the pile merely trembled, the child calmly waited for the movement to stop and then proceeded with the construction of his column. But if the trembling caused the pile to fall, the child almost invariably reacted by pressing his button and trying to make another child's pile fall.

In other laboratory tests of frustration, college students were kept awake all night, promised food, entertainment and cigarettes, and then were denied all of these rewards when they were weary; all became irritable and angry, and one showed his frustration by drawing grotesque caricatures of human figures that had been stabbed, bloodied and hanged. When asked what the pictures represented, the student exclaimed, "Psychologists!" All these tests proved plainly enough that aggressive responses can be provoked by frustration; but from nursery to college, the nature of the response varied with the age and sophistication of the subjects.

Animal experimenters suggest that the response varies in terms of the accessibility of the goal. Nathan Azrin found after training pigeons to peck a key for the reward of grain, and then withdrawing the grain, that the birds became agitated and flapped around the cage. If nothing happened, a frustrated pigeon would eventually give up and subside into apathy. But if it was provided with a target, such as another pigeon (alive or even stuffed), the frustrated pigeon would attack it. And if provided with no target unless and until it pecked another key, which released the target, the pigeon would peck that key to get at the target as vigorously as it had pecked the first key to get the grain. In other words, some sort of goal or substitute must be discernible to a subject if aggression is to occur.

Other experiments, carried out with people, have indicated that the nearer the goal, the more violent is the aggressive response when the goal is made unobtainable. Psychologist Mary Harris put this to the test in a place where every contemporary grocery shopper has experienced frustration of one sort or another—the supermarket checkout counter. At a supermarket crowded with shoppers pushing carts loaded with groceries, Harris or one of her confederates broke into the checkout line, sometimes in front of the person whose turn was next, sometimes in the middle of the line, sometimes near the tail end. The shoppers reacted with varying degrees of aggression by shoving the psychologist's cart out of line and insisting on keeping their position, by shouting abuse or by glaring silently.

However, the vehemence with which they made these aggressive responses depended on where the customers were standing in the line. The most aggressive of all were the shoppers who were nearest the front of the line; the least aggressive were those in the rear. The shoppers at the front were impatient, aroused from having endured a long wait; equally important, they were nearer to their goal—the cash register and the completion of their task. The ones at the end of the line had the same goal, but having queued up only a moment or two before, they expected to have a long wait, and in a line that stretched far in front of them, one shopping cart more or less did not constitute such an obvious interference with their goal.

When the goal seems so distant that it may never be achieved, frustration may produce a lack of aggression. This fact helps explain an anomaly in the incidence of homicides in the United States. In prosperous times the proportion of murders in which whites kill whites goes down, and in bad times it goes up. But the rate for homicides in which blacks murder blacks goes in the opposite direction.

One psychologist attributed the phenomenon to the differences in the goals and expectations of whites and blacks. In times of plenty, the argument goes, whites generally expect to get ahead, and enough of them do so to make the goal seem reachable for all. In a depression, whites who have suffered economic setbacks keep as their goals the success of those fellow whites who have remained well off, not others who, like themselves, have lost out; they therefore consider themselves to be cut off from an achievable goal, economic progress. The frustration arouses their aggressiveness so much that they readily turn to homicide. For blacks, on the other hand, it is prosperity, not depression, that creates a great disparity in the accessibility of goals. Prosperity raises the expectations of all but not all fulfill these raised expectations; those who are left behind are the ones who suffer frustrations. During a depression, however, blacks lose their jobs in great numbers. Most blacks are in the same predicament: few expect much, and they therefore do not feel any resentment toward one another. Hence, the homicide rate among blacks goes down.

In a similar fashion, revolutions occur most often not in societies where political and economic conditions are unrelievedly bad, but in societies where there is some expectation, however illusory, of improvement. That is one reason why South Africa remained relatively quiet during the 1960s while the cities of the United States were beset with riots. In South Africa blacks had been oppressed by whites for so long that they had no memory of better times past, and no expectation of better times to come. In the United States, on the other hand, the national ethic had long held out the promise of social and economic opportunity for people of all backgrounds. For American blacks, those promises took on new meaning with the economic expansion that followed the Second World War, and their hopes were buoyed by the civil rights legislation passed during the early 1960s. But as the goals came closer, the potential for frustration increased. When, toward the end of the 1960s, it appeared that most blacks were still unfairly barred from the economic and political advancement that had been promised, anger mounted. All that was needed to detonate violence was a trigger.

The trigger that touches off aggression is simply the event that releases emotional arousal, converting it into an explosion of violence. The trigger may be totally removed from whatever caused arousal, and may have nothing to do with frustration, pain or threat. A heedless remark from a bystander frequently triggers aggression. And sometimes the presence of a target or weapon triggers aggression. More often, however, the trigger is further arousal: the final, unendurable step in a long series of incidents that already have brought the individual to the verge of aggression.

Such was the case in France in 1968, when a series of frustrations mounted and spread, so arousing the populace that only a minor incident was needed to trigger violence. The event that served as the trigger was the closing down, for budgetary reasons, of the Nanterre campus of

continued on page 99

Expecting trouble, police watchfully eye fans arriving for a soccer match between the Manchester United and Cardiff City teams.

The soccer hooligans of Merrie England

Great Britain is known as a peaceful, law-abiding land, yet beginning in the late 1960s it fell victim to outbreaks of a special kind of violence—soccer hooliganism. Soccer matches, immensely popular in Britain, were turned into mass brawls as gangs of toughs attacked rival groups of fans, fought police, wrecked stadiums, buses and trains, and terrified the inhabitants of the cities where the matches were held.

The hooligans were youths in their teens or early twenties who held frustrating blue-collar jobs, often drank heavily and expressed their aggressiveness at soccer matches. In team colors, they crammed the stadiums, swaying rhythmically and waving scarves while hurling insults at rival groups. At the game between Manchester United and Cardiff City in September 1974, for example, Welsh Cardiff fans jeered, "Munich '58," referring to a plane crash that had killed eight Manchester players. The Manchester fans screamed, "Aberfan!"—the name of the Welsh village where 116 children and 28 adults died in a coal-slag avalanche.

In such an incendiary atmosphere —made more combustible by consumption of huge amounts of alcohol and frequent confrontations with police— only a spark was needed to turn verbal aggression into full-scale violence.

Fans and police confront each other at the 1975 European Cup Final in Paris, helping trigger violence that ended in $200,000 damage and an apology to the French from the British Ambassador.

Angered by a goal scored by the opposing Manchester City team, Manchester United fans rush onto the field, spoiling for a fight. Police tried vainly to turn back the hooligans; an all-out battle ensued.

*Trapped in a surging crowd at Tottenham
Hotspur's ground in London, a lone
policeman is mauled by angry soccer fans.*

*Police forcibly remove a hooligan
at a particularly explosive match between
Manchester United and Cardiff City.*

the University of Paris, a step that might have passed without incident in other circumstances.

For the students, this action was one frustration too many. For months they had been grumbling about a scarcity of teachers, overloaded classes and an outdated curriculum. Space in lecture halls, for instance, was so inadequate that students had to arrive an hour in advance to make sure of a seat; they often sat through a lecture in a field they were not even studying in order to be present when their own turn came.

Students responded to the Nanterre shutdown by organizing a demonstration, which began peaceably enough but turned unruly when some protesters seized a campus building. The government sent out the police, who rushed onto the campus swinging clubs and firing tear gas to quell the disorder.

Such forceful suppression of protest brought a public outcry that intensified and widened the dispute. At the time all France was aroused by frustrating annoyances: inflation, high taxes and the frictions of the authoritarian rule of President Charles de Gaulle. Middle-class Parisian workers took to the streets to demonstrate in sympathy with the students; and, surprisingly, labor unions—ordinarily aloof from student affairs—responded with a series of wildcat strikes, first in Paris and its suburbs, then spreading from one town to another across France. Soon auto workers, construction crews, garbage collectors and mailmen stopped work. Subway transportation, food-market operations and banking came to a halt, and such basic necessities as household heat, electricity and water were curtailed.

The result was a national strike in which nearly 10 million workers participated, paralyzing the whole of France for more than a month. The country was so aroused that once the initial trigger, the closing of the Nanterre campus, had released violence, that incident triggered another (the government's dispatching of the police) and another (demonstrations by the general populace) and another, and so on.

Psychologists call this phenomenon a "contagion of violence." The 19th Century French sociologist Gabriel Tarde was among the first to recognize it. He made the observation that epidemics of crime "follow the line of the telegraph," pointing out that immediately after London had buzzed with sensational stories about Jack the Ripper and his victims, a sudden rash of crimes involving the brutal mutilation and murder of women occurred all over the English countryside. Overnight the telegraph had carried information that, before its invention, would have traveled at the leisurely pace of storytelling—and perhaps would have lost virulence as it lost immediacy.

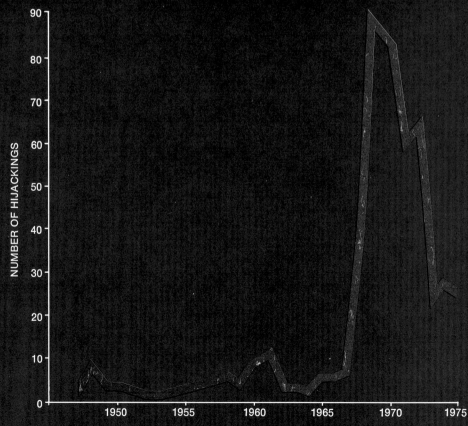

A swift contagion of hijacking

On an airfield in Rome, above, one man lies dead and two others are hustled off at gunpoint by a terrorist hijacking the airliner behind them during a flurry of hijacking that struck in 1967. The epidemic's rise and fall, graphed at right, indicates the infectious nature of aggression; other crimes given wide publicity—such as the kidnappings in the 1970s—follow a similar pattern.

Air piracy broke out after World War II among refugees escaping Communist governments in Eastern Europe, increased briefly after the Castro takeover in Cuba, but remained generally rare. Then the idea suddenly spread, inciting a wave of hijackings by terrorists, dissidents, misfits and extortionists. The epidemic subsided as abruptly as it began. Despite brief resurgences in 1970 and 1974, it was brought under control by strict security measures.

NUMBER OF HIJACKINGS

90
80
70
60
50
40
30
20
10
0

1950   1955   1960   1965   1970   1975

In the 1970s, when television was spreading news far faster than the telegraph, new instances of contagions of violence occurred whose effects were felt worldwide. There were epidemics of airplane hijackings *(chart, left)*, and kidnappings resulted in the abduction of 41 people in Italy in a single year, 96 in the United States and over 500 in Argentina. So acute was the situation in Argentina that at some of the more elegant parties in an affluent Buenos Aires suburb, as many as a third of the people who were present were bodyguards, hired by anxious hosts to protect the safety of their guests.

Whatever the source of arousal, and whatever the trigger that detonates the explosion, every act of human aggression requires a weapon. A sharp tongue and a clenched fist may serve as weapons of a sort in some disputes. But what gives human aggression special horror is that unlike animals, which fight only with the claws and the teeth with which nature endowed them, human beings use tools: the club, the knife, the missile, the gun, even the car. Such weapons as these raise the human potential for violence to lethal proportions. Not only do they make destruction more certain and the aggressor's job easier, but they also remove the aggressor psychologically from the damage he inflicts and reduce emotional inhibitions against violence. Thus weapons do more than serve as essential instruments; they may be causes of violence, arousing and triggering it.

The easy accessibility of guns in the United States is frequently cited as a cause of the nation's high murder rate. The United States is one of the few industrialized countries that allow almost anyone to own a gun. More than half of American homes have at least one rifle, pistol or shotgun. Understandably, a large number of deaths and injuries result. Many of them are accidents or suicides, but in 1974 the United States had 12,474 murders by gunfire, over 170 times as many as occurred in Japan, where only the police and the armed forces are permitted to keep guns, and over 1,500 times as many as in Britain, where not even policemen carry guns.

But the danger in guns may well be a subtler matter than the number of gun victims. An experiment by psychologist Leonard Berkowitz has raised the possibility that guns may even trigger violence with other kinds of weapons. "What I suspect is that in a very real sense the presence of the gun might inflame the individual," Berkowitz theorizes, "because he looks at the gun and recognizes it as an aggressive object. And that stirs him so that, in a sense, he has become more disposed to violence than he would have been if he hadn't seen the gun."

In testing his hypothesis in his laboratory at the University of Wis-

Carbine ammunition is the featured special of the day in a California sporting goods store during the explosive riots in Watts in 1965.

The double-barreled threat of the gun

Lax gun laws make it astonishingly easy to buy these deadly weapons in the United States, as the scene above demonstrates. As a result, there are more guns in the United States—approximately 135 million, or two for every household—than anywhere else. Moreover, they represent a dual threat. Guns make violence more deadly simply because it is so much easier to kill a person with a gun than with bare hands or a club—an average of 20,000 people are shot to death each year in the United States. In addition, guns may make violence of all kinds more likely to occur.

This conclusion is suggested by a study designed by psychologist Leonard Berkowitz of the University of Wiscon-

sin, which involved 100 students. Some of the students were angry, and some were not. Some of each group were shown the guns and some were not. All of the students then were told to administer shocks to their colleagues. The students who were angry and who were also shown the guns administered the heaviest shocks.

Berkowitz's results indicate that the mere sight of a gun raises the level of aggression of people who are already aroused. And that may help to explain why the United States—where so many guns are in evidence—leads the industrialized world in homicides committed not only with guns, but with other weapons as well.

consin, Berkowitz's approach was to arouse a number of subjects to anger with mild electric shocks. Then he provided them with what they thought was the chance to shock the experimenting psychologist in return. Half the subjects got this chance while seated at a table on which a collection of innocuous objects such as badminton rackets and shuttlecocks lay next to the key they would press to deliver the fake shocks. The other half were seated at a table containing a shotgun and a revolver. Berkowitz found that the subjects who saw the guns were much more ready to deliver shocks to the psychologist than those who saw only the badminton gear.

In interviews afterward, the subjects denied that the guns had influenced their feelings of anger or their urge to press the shock key. But the fact that they were unaware of the guns' influence makes it all the more insidious. "The finger pulls the trigger," Berkowitz wrote, "but the trigger may also be pulling the finger."

A less obvious but handier weapon for aggression is that ubiquitous means of everyday transportation: the automobile. Cars are so commonplace in daily life that they are seldom thought of as weapons for aggression. But the fact is that more people die violent deaths in automobiles than from any other cause except organized warfare. In England and Wales, with a total population of over 49 million, there were 6,869 deaths by motor vehicles in 1972. In the United States, with a population of more than 211 million, there were 56,300 fatalities. Furthermore, a surprising proportion of these fatalities were the victims of aggression. For the word accident is generally used to describe these incidents, but to the extent that "accident" suggests mere chance, it may be misleading.

Psychiatrist Van Buren Hammett, who studied drivers on American roads, supported this conclusion. "The automobile is particularly well adapted for the expression of aggression," Hammett said. "The driver needs only to press lightly with his foot upon the accelerator (an act which requires no more force than that necessary to pull the trigger of a revolver) and by so doing, he can propel an object of great mass at high speed. This can be done as effectively by the small and weak as the large and strong, so that the modern automobile when used is an even more potent equalizer than the Colt 45 of Western Frontier days."

Hammett and his colleagues spent 34 days observing drivers on Pennsylvania's commuter highways. And while they witnessed no collisions during that period, they reported 100 "clearcut instances of aggressive driving," including such overtly aggressive behavior as weaving, cutting across in front of other cars, tailgating and racing. British

psychologist M. H. Parry, in interviews with hundreds of randomly selected British motorists, found that most accidents are caused by drivers
in just such a state of anxiety as was experienced by the British clerk
who rammed his automobile into the one in front of him. Among the
most alarming of Parry's findings was that 15 per cent of the men he
studied confessed to feeling murderous impulses while driving on the
highway, while 13 per cent said they had actually come to physical
blows with other drivers. Almost all of the men and women reported
swearing at other drivers, making obscene gestures, as well as engaging
in malicious horn honking and tailgating.

Far from being violence prone, the drivers were normal, nonaggressive, good citizens at home, at work and virtually everywhere except behind the wheel. People who "scorn the growth of social violence," Parry
concluded, "change into selfish, aggressive and dangerous beings in the
time it takes to get into and start a car." This occurs most often, no
doubt, when the drivers are aroused to anger before they start the car.
Then, when triggered to violence by some incident on the road, they
have a lethal weapon—the car—in their hands.

Given the proper degree of arousal, the trigger and the weapon, there
remains one other factor necessary to aggression, and that is the target.
The nature of the target, especially in the mind of the aggressor, has a
great deal to do with whether or not aggression occurs, and if it does,
what form it takes.

Sometimes a target can serve as the trigger that sets off aggression, as
in the case of someone whose mere name or face—or sex—is enough to
make another person see red. The woman driver—not only in the minds
of men, but also in the minds of other women—has always been the butt
of jokes and cartoons. Psychologists' experiments have borne out the not-
so-humorous feelings that underlie the jokes; they have demonstrated
that when an automobile is stalled in traffic, people who would not ordinarily act violently toward a woman are much more likely to honk their
horns aggressively if the stalled car is driven by a woman than if it is
driven by a man.

This readiness to behave aggressively toward women drivers is an
anomaly. Outside of driving, people are much less likely to be aggressive against a woman target than against a man. Middle-class boys are
taught as they are growing up that it is cowardly to attack women and
girls—and indeed most refrain from doing so, even when there is provocation. When psychologist Mary Harris' experiment aroused unsuspecting shoppers by breaking into the queue at a supermarket checkout
counter, for example, the frustrated customers regularly spoke up in

anger when a male experimenter broke into line ahead of them but rarely did so when a woman broke in.

In addition to sex, the economic or social status of an individual may also make him more—or less—inviting as a target. Psychologists Anthony Doob and Alan E. Gross turned to the automobile again to demonstrate this fact. They observed drivers' reactions to an experimenter's car deliberately stalled in front of them. They found that when the experimenter wore an old khaki jacket and drove a small economy car, other drivers were half again as likely to honk their horns as they were when he wore a plaid sports jacket over a white shirt and drove an expensive sedan.

The result observed in this experiment was the same whether the drivers happened to be men or women. Yet attitudes toward this kind of situation seemed to depend strikingly on sex, as Doob and Gross discovered when they went back to the classroom and asked students—men and women not involved in the previous experiment—how they would react if they found themselves behind a stalled car. The answers given by the men were opposite to those given by the women. The female students said they would do what the experiment had shown actually happened —honk at the smaller car and not at the larger one. The male students said they would do what the men observed did not do—honk at the larger car—perhaps because of an inner need to present a masculine image of standing up to a powerful adversary.

The behavior of the target will also influence an aggressor's action. A study of homicides in Philadelphia showed that more than one fourth of the killers had been provoked by the victim, and criminologists maintain that in many violent crimes the victim's actions actually help to spur the aggressor.

Hans Toch, investigating encounters between police and civilians, found that some policemen unwittingly trigger violence, escalating trivial incidents by asserting their authority so ineptly they provoke assault. Toch quoted a boy who had been charged with striking a policeman as saying, "I'm thinking to myself, you know, 'this is a dumb cop.' " By expressing this attitude the boy provoked the policeman and made an inviting target of himself. As the policeman explained the incident, "I hear him yell something about, 'You're going to die,' or some stupid thing. He had yelled something that in my opinion was a threat to my life." In this case, violence occurred because each participant made himself an inviting target for the other's anger.

In many instances of aggression, the target turns out to be extremely elusive. Then the mechanism Freud called "displacement" may come into play: a substitute target is found and aggression is diverted to it.

A form of displacement familiar to almost everyone is the sudden explosion of fury, for no apparent reason, at anyone who happens to become available. A worker suffers a reprimand from his boss, for example. He does not fight back for various reasons: partly for fear of losing his job, but partly also because his prior training is likely to have given him inhibitions against committing aggression against those having authority over him. He smolders all day, and then when he gets home in a high state of arousal, an irritating remark by his wife triggers him and he explodes.

Some instances of displacement are more virulent—and harder to identify. The bizarre and deadly practice of lynching was sometimes a form of displacement. Psychologists Carl Hovland and Robert Sears examined 4,761 recorded lynchings, mostly of blacks, that took place in the American South between 1882 and 1930. They found that the rate of lynching varied inversely with the price of cotton, then the mainstay of the South's economy.

When times were bad, the price of cotton dropped and the frequency of lynchings soared. The victims of the lynchings had nothing to do with the mobs' real grievance: a scarcity of jobs. But there was nothing that wage earners could do about the unemployment caused by the drop in the price of cotton. They felt unable to express their frustrations by assaulting the immediate source of their distress, the millowners who had discharged them. So they found other targets—convicted or suspected criminals, most of whom were blacks, and all of whom could be attacked with impunity. Such are the grisly lengths to which human aggression can go, particularly, it appears, when individual frustrations are shared by people in groups.

Danger in Numbers

4

On the evening of March 5, 1770, a young American colonist insulted the British sentry at the Custom House in Boston, and the Redcoat retaliated by bashing the American on the side of the head with his musket. The skirmish attracted a crowd to the Custom House, and violence spread like a contagion. People began cursing the sentry and throwing snowballs at him. A relief detail came out to the sentry's aid, and a chorus of colonists taunted the British soldiers, daring them to fire. One of the Redcoats was knocked to the ground; he got up in a rage and fired his musket into the crowd. The colonists closed in, and the violence escalated irreversibly as more shots were fired.

The incident scarcely deserved the title Boston Massacre accorded it by history—just five colonists were killed—but it helped ignite the American Revolution, which erupted five years later, and it says a great deal about violence and aggression involving large numbers of people. For the episode might have ended almost where it began but for one enormously significant fact: the antagonists were members of groups, and violence involving groups is almost always more volatile than clashes between individuals. This is true whether the participants are colonists and Redcoats, or Japanese students confronting a phalanx of helmeted policemen in the streets of Tokyo *(left)*. The potential for violence is greater not only because there are more combatants to harm one another but also because people behave differently in groups. They are willing to perform acts of aggression and violence that in other circumstances would be abhorrent to them.

Not all groups are violent, of course. People get together for concerts, meetings, nonviolent demonstrations and other peaceful purposes. However, simply dividing people into groups or categories intensifies their feelings and their behavior. "If they are feeling pleasant they are likely to be more pleasant," commented one psychologist, "and if they are feeling violent or ugly, they are likely to be more violent or ugly."

Membership in the group serves not only to intensify the feelings of individuals, but also to make it more likely these feelings will be translated into action. If those in a group are prone to violence, they are more likely to behave violently because of the multiple effects of group membership. For the group provides them a protective cloak of anonymity that makes them feel freer to commit violence and less likely to be punished or feel guilty if they do. Membership in the group also serves to legitimize the violence, providing a rationale for it in terms of service to a higher cause. It produces pressures on the individual to conform to the group's code of behavior, to obey its authority and to participate in acts of aggression against the objects of its prejudices and hatreds. All these factors not only increase the likelihood of violence and aggression but also magnify its effects once it occurs.

Group membership influences violence so much because it confers anonymity. Psychologists call the process "deindividuation"—the submerging of individuality in the group. As Jonathan Freedman, J. Merrill Carlsmith and David Sears explain the process in their analysis: "Individuals lose their personal sense of responsibility when they are in a group. Instead of feeling, as they usually do, that they personally are morally accountable for their actions, group members somehow share the responsibility with one another, and none of them feels it as strongly as he would if he were alone." This relaxation of self-restraint has a decisive effect on behavior. "The more anonymous the group members are," Freedman and his associates say, "the less they feel they have an identity of their own, and the more irresponsibly they may behave."

Sometimes a group will take unusual pains to make certain its members are equally guilty and equally innocent. A dramatic example of this occurred in Mississippi in 1964 after the slaying of three civil rights workers. According to some reports, the slayers passed the murder weapon from hand to hand so each would feel equally responsible and yet none would be individually guilty.

A similar sharing of responsibility is generally institutionalized in the rituals surrounding executions. At an electrocution three executioners pull separate switches, but only one switch actually opens the lethal current. In death by firing squad it is customary for one of the rifles to be loaded with blanks so that each squad member can believe he bears no personal responsibility. In fact, most decision-making systems such as government bureaucracies are structured in such a way that they diffuse and obscure individual responsibility. Even the grammar of certain languages provides for diffusion of responsibility. In Japanese, one verb form enables the speaker to disclaim his own action—instead of saying, "I will not fight," he says, "I don't want to be made to fight."

The most effective way to lose one's identity is to cover it up. The mere fact of membership in a large group or crowd tends to make people feel faceless, but deindividuation is greatly enhanced when distinctive personal characteristics such as name, face or even dress are obscured besides.

How such anonymity of individual members promotes aggression was demonstrated by Philip Zimbardo in a series of experiments with female students at New York University. When the women arrived at Zimbardo's laboratory for the experiment, half of them were asked to don hoods and large shapeless laboratory coats. The names of those in this group were never used and neither the other subjects nor the experimenters themselves could tell one from another. They were the anonymous group. The other subjects were identifiable; they were greeted by name as they arrived, wore badges bearing their names and generally had their personal identity emphasized throughout the study.

Like most psychological experiments, it was disguised with a fictitious purpose. The cover story was complicated but the upshot was simple. When the anonymous subjects were given the opportunity to deliver what they thought were electric shocks to a female victim, they were nearly twice as aggressive as the identifiable ones. In Zimbardo's words, "These sweet, normally mild-mannered college girls shocked another girl almost every time they had an opportunity to do so, sometimes for as long as they were allowed, and it did not matter whether or not that fellow student was a nice girl who didn't deserve to be hurt."

Zimbardo attempted to repeat his anonymity experiment in Belgium at the University of Louvain, using Belgian soldiers from a nearby base. But this time the results were reversed: the hooded soldiers delivered less shock punishment to a victim than did soldiers who were identifiable. A clue to the reason was revealed in answers to postexperiment questionnaires. The soldiers who were supposed to be anonymous felt different from their army buddies because of their hoods. All of the soldiers in the experiment were accustomed to wearing uniforms and to the anonymity of army life. They were already depersonalized when they arrived for the experiment. But, by making some of them wear hoods, the experimenters made them feel self-conscious, suspicious and anxious. Instead of feeling anonymous, they stuck out—and their aggressiveness was inhibited instead of being increased.

Zimbardo's investigations turned up another variation of the effect of group anonymity. He discovered that when people merge their identities with groups, their aggressiveness is determined to some extent by

what they think is expected of them. In this experiment, Zimbardo and his colleagues converted a basement at Stanford University into a make-believe prison and randomly assigned student volunteers the roles of prisoners and guards.

The "prisoners" were rounded up in realistic raids at their homes or dormitories, fingerprinted, searched, photographed and handcuffed by a real policeman. At the "prison" the make-believe guards took over. They wore identical uniforms of khaki shirts and pants and had on silvered sunglasses—the kind that are transparent to the wearer but opaque from the outside—to prevent eye contact with the prisoners. To ensure feelings of anonymity, the prisoners were also outfitted in identical stocking caps and smocks with stenciled numbers.

Both guards and prisoners played their roles so convincingly that it soon became impossible for observers to distinguish the play acting from reality. The subjects conformed to their society's—and hence their own—expectations of what was appropriate for each group: prisoners ought to be servile, passive, less than human; guards ought to be authoritarian, tough, even brutal. The guards kept their charges in line with night sticks and, when prisoners rebelled, with streams of chilling foam from fire extinguishers. To amuse themselves, they stretched the routine 10-minute prisoner count into hours, created useless make-work, such as picking thorns out of blankets, and encouraged prisoners to vilify one another. Five prisoners developed real symptoms of anxiety, such as depression, uncontrollable crying and fits of rage, and had to be released. The experiment had been scheduled to run two weeks but the effect on the subjects was so severely cruel, it was ended after six days.

The merging of identities with a group not only increases the possibility of violence, but it also sometimes prevents well-meaning people from coming to the aid of the victims. In New York, an 18-year-old switchboard operator was raped and beaten in her office. She escaped and ran naked and bleeding into the street, screaming for help. On the sidewalk about 40 bystanders gathered and watched while the rapist tried to drag her back into the office. Two policemen who happened by rescued the woman, but no one in the crowd had moved to help her.

Bystanders' refusal to intervene on behalf of people in distress has been attributed to a myriad of modern psychic ailments—alienation, apathy and indifference. Indeed, some psychiatrists have said the failure to help stems from unconscious sadism, which itself would constitute a form of passive aggression against the victim. But psychologists John Darley, of New York University, and Bibb Latané, of Columbia University, offered a different explanation. They suspected that group anonymity could relieve each member of responsibility for reacting to violence as he ordinarily might. He might not even interpret the situation as an emergency unless he saw evidence that someone else was taking it seriously. This thesis was later tested in an experiment conducted by Latané with fellow psychologist Judith Rodin and appropriately titled "A Lady in Distress." A woman experimenter asked the subjects to fill out a questionnaire, then disappeared into the next room. A few minutes later the subjects could hear from the next room unmistakable sounds of her distress: a chair collapsing, moans and agonized cries of "O, my God, my foot . . . my ankle . . . I can't get this thing off me."

If the subject was alone when he heard these expressions of pain, he offered to help the experimenter in 70 per cent of the cases. But if the subjects were in pairs, only 20 per cent offered help. Interviews afterward explained why: despite the evidence of his own ears, a subject tended to take his cues about what was happening from the other member of the group. In the presence of others, the individual usually tried to appear calm when confronted with an emergency. Thus, Darley and Latané concluded, each member of the experimental pairs conformed to the other's apparent lack of concern.

In another experiment Darley and Latané found that anonymity inspired a diffusion of responsibility even if the group was scattered. Bystanders who witness distress from separate vantage points, they suggested, may not feel personally accountable because they automatically assume someone else is aiding the victim, even though they cannot tell that help is indeed being offered. Darley and Latané placed subjects alone in separate rooms, but provided them with an intercom so they could communicate with one another if necessary. Over the intercom, subjects heard one of the participants (actually an accomplice of the experimenter) suffer an apparent epileptic seizure. If the subject thought he was the only one tuned in on the seizure, he was likely to leave his room and try to help the apparent victim. But if he thought others be-

side himself knew of the emergency, he was less ready to act. The greater the number of other subjects he thought were listening, the less likely he was to try to help.

To confirm these results outside the laboratory, Darley and Latané staged a make-believe crime wave at a suburban store whose owner agreed to cooperate. In a two-week period, the store was "robbed" 96 times by accomplices of the experimenters—two husky students dressed in rough clothes. The store's cashier played his role by walking to a back room while the thieves made off with a case of beer. The action was timed so that either one or two unwitting customers were present to witness the apparent theft. If two witnesses were present, they were far less likely to report the crime to the cashier than was one witness alone. Even in such small groups, members tended to conform to others' behavior and not feel personally responsible.

When an individual covers his own identity with that of a group, his actions gain a legitimacy they would not otherwise have because he acts under the cloak of group motivations. They are often different from those of an individual. The individual who commits an act of aggression on his own usually does so for personal or selfish reasons—to achieve a specific reward or simply to release anger. But when the individual becomes a member of a group, his motives and emotions transcend the self. He and his group commit violence for a higher cause. Whether the higher cause is the true religion, a political ideology or loyalty to race or flag, its effect can be galvanic. "Never is evil done so thoroughly or so well," wrote the 17th Century French philosopher Blaise Pascal, "as when it is done in a good cause."

Service to a cause requires the surrender of independence. Every member of the group is expected to obey its command. This simple concept, obedience to authority, probably has justified more violence than any other idea in the world. Over the 10,000-year history of organized warfare, soldiers have unhesitatingly maimed and killed people in obedience to some authority in their group—the sergeant, general or national leader. They were simply following orders. In such a case, everyday standards of right and wrong and even of sanity might become irrelevant. As an old Ukranian proverb puts it, "When the banner is unfurled, all reason is in the trumpet."

A mass murderer like Adolf Eichmann could try to justify the Germans' slaughter of six million Jews during the Second World War on the grounds that he was merely doing his duty as a member of a group. Terrorists have hijacked planes, assassinated government officials and set off murderous bombs—not for personal gain, but in obedience

In an act of savage violence, a Bangladesh soldier bayonets a Pakistani captive to death during the postwar vengeance that followed the conflict in 1972. Such extreme brutality is more likely when a person acts in the name of a group than when he acts on his own because, psychologists say, of deindividuation. He surrenders his identity and his sense of personal responsibility to the discipline and objectives of the group.

These extraordinary photographs confirm a startling research finding: several bystanders are less likely to aid a victim of violence than is a lone spectator. At top, two of a group of onlookers watch as a mugger knocks a man down. They do not even take their hands from their pockets (center) as the intended victim begins to chase his assailant. And when the victim draws a knife and lunges toward the mugger (bottom), the crowd makes no move to intervene.

to the authority of political factions, ethnic groups or religions.

In most cases the killers bore their victims no personal animosity. During the Christmas truce of World War I, for example, British and German soldiers could emerge from the trenches, shake hands and swap mementos before the fighting resumed. During World War II, the novelist George Orwell noted with detachment: "As I write, highly civilized human beings are flying overhead, trying to kill me. They do not feel any enmity against me as an individual, nor I against them. They are only 'doing their duty' as the saying goes."

That obedience to authority is a deeply ingrained human response, overriding normal considerations of sympathy and ethics, was vividly demonstrated by the notorious "Eichmann Experiment," conducted by psychologist Stanley Milgram at Yale University in the early 1960s. Milgram set out to measure the obedience of subjects who were ordered by a legitimate authority to harm another human being. To disguise the purpose of his experiment, Milgram created an elaborate fiction. He told his volunteer subjects they were participating in research that would test the effects of punishment on the rate of a fellow subject's learning. Each subject was to administer electric shocks of progressively greater intensity to the learner for each successive wrong answer to a test; the shocks were nonexistent, but the subject did not know that because the learner—an accomplice of Milgram's—reacted as if he had been hurt.

Originally, Milgram had suspected that the teachings of a culture would influence the results; he thought some national groups—Germans, especially—would be inclined toward conformity and obedience. He expected Americans—indoctrinated in the value of independence, self-reliance and personal responsibility—to be reluctant to obey orders violating the dictates of conscience. He assumed that not many would be willing to go so far as to administer the highest, most painful voltage to the victim. His fellow scientists made the same assumption. Indeed, before the experiment, many behavioral scientists had predicted that no more than a pathological fringe of 1 or 2 per cent would be willing to press the button for the greatest shocks. Astonishingly, 65 per cent of the subjects—teachers, salesmen, laborers, clerks—did so. To Milgram the result showed how "ordinary people, simply doing their jobs, and without any particular hostility, can become agents in a terrible destructive process." The basic experiment has been repeated in Germany, Italy, South Africa and Australia, and to some extent Milgram's expectations were borne out: in each of these countries the level of obedience was somewhat higher than in the United States. (In Germany, 85 per cent of the subjects were willing to apply maximum voltage.)

Milgram's work stirred a furor. Critics charged that Milgram, by subjecting his volunteers to emotional strain under false pretenses, was himself guilty of brutality.

The controversy has tended to obscure some remarkable additional findings reported by Milgram in his book *Obedience to Authority*. These findings, which show how varying circumstances can affect obedience, were made possible by the experiment's standardized design. The basic experiment and each variation called for 40 subjects—a sampling balanced for a range of ages and occupations (except in one variation, all the subjects were male). This plan enabled Milgram to compare obedience responses under a variety of conditions. For example, in a bureaucratic situation—the subject did not press the shock button him-

Protected behind bulletproof glass at his 1961 trial on charges of overseeing the Nazi extermination of six million Jews, Adolf Eichmann enters a plea that is a common justification for violence by members of a group: obedience to orders. "I was a tool," he said, "in the hands of superior powers and authorities."

self but merely asked the test questions while a laboratory assistant pressed the button for wrong answers—92.5 per cent continued to participate as the voltage was increased to the maximum. But if the subject was given free rein to choose any shock level, only 2.5 per cent selected the highest voltage.

Other experiments varied the proximity of the subject to the man who issued the orders or to the victim. When the orders were issued over the telephone, instead of in person, obedience plummeted to 20.5 per cent. Interestingly, several subjects secretly disobeyed telephone orders by consistently using only the lowest shock level. They were willing to undermine the experiment, but they were not willing to make an open break with authority.

Varying the proximity of subject and victim had a reverse effect: the closer the victim intruded upon the consciousness—and conscience—of the subject, the lower the obedience level. One variation made the victim's suffering audible, keying his protests to the rising shock intensity —a grunt, then groans, the cry, "Experimenter, get me out of here!," an agonized scream, and finally ominous silence. Hearing this litany of agony, subjects nonetheless were 62.5 per cent obedient. But when the victim was in the room and thus in view, obedience dropped to 40 per cent. And when subjects had to touch the victim by forcing his hand onto the shock plate, 30 per cent were willing to escalate the pain to the top voltage level.

Similarly, the remoteness of suffering in modern push-button warfare makes it easier for an individual to carry out the dictates of his group. Psychiatrist Robert Jay Lifton pointed out that interviews with American pilots during the Vietnam War revealed a parallel to the Milgram experiments—the greater the aircraft's altitude, the less a pilot's apparent feelings of guilt. Talking about their jobs, high-flying B-52 pilots, who saw the destruction they wrought as blips on a radar screen, spoke only of professional skill and performance. Fighter-bomber pilots, who caught glimpses of the people on the ground, felt compelled to rationalize the killing. And the pilots of helicopter gunships, who saw everything close up, expressed the same feelings of emotional conflict that beset many ground troops.

"As for the man who sits in front of a button that will release Armageddon," Milgram noted, "depressing it has about the same emotional force as calling for an elevator." Yet in his own subjects the emotional tug of war between conscience and obedience was poignantly evident. Some of the subjects sweated, trembled, stuttered, bit their lips, groaned. Others suffered fits of nervous laughter. One of

A grinning mob surrounds its victims after a lynching. In the United States such group aggression, directed mainly at blacks, took the lives of more than 3,400 between 1882 and 1951. Though lynch mobs were motivated primarily by racial prejudices, a 1933 study showed that economic frustration was an important factor in triggering the violence.

them, a social worker, would burst into laughter upon hearing the learner's screams. Still others found ways of lessening the strain by protesting that they were not responsible for the victim's suffering or by trying to tip him off to right answers to the learning test so that he would not have to suffer. And many, like the B-52 pilots, found refuge in the mechanics of their task. They pressed the buttons with great care and read the words of the learning test with exaggerated articulation—loudly, to drown out the victim's protests.

Willingness to obey orders is one aspect of conformity. This cohesive force serves a dual purpose: it melds diverse individuals into a group, and once bound together, it enables them to act in concert. Conformity does not require orders. So powerful is the urge to conform that, in laboratory experiments, many people automatically attempt to express what they perceive as the consensus of their group. They refute the evidence of their own eyes or ears and go along with the majority —even if the majority is obviously wrong. This result has been obtained in experiments in France, Norway and the United States.

Nowhere perhaps was the tendency to go along with the group more dramatically demonstrated than in the notorious American slaughter of civilians in My Lai during the Vietnam War. A number of reasons help account for the behavior of the American soldiers at My Lai—the stress of combat, prejudice against the Vietnamese, and obedience to authority. But once the massacre had begun, the soldiers were under heavy pressure to conform. So great was this pressure to go along with the group that the handful of soldiers who refused to fire at civilians hid that fact from their fellows. One shot himself in the foot to avoid participation in the killings.

The great question raised by such horrors, of course, is: why are people so willing to follow group behavior when their actions result in terrible harm to others? The most compelling reason is the fear of being labeled deviant. People who deviate from group behavior are themselves frequent targets of aggression. The renegade, in fact, may suffer more hostility than the group's outside enemies. His deviance threatens the values of the group—and sometimes its survival. An extreme example of the reaction to the threat of deviance is the treatment accorded a traitor to his country, but a more familiar instance is the hostility that greets deviance from such everyday standards as codes of dress and even hair styles.

During the 1960s long hair was considered deviant in many countries, not only because it was different, but also because it came to symbolize a larger departure from accepted behavior: antiwar protest and rebellion against middle-class life styles. Long hair and the ideas it symbolized triggered various forms of aggression. People cursed it, schools outlawed it. In New York, construction workers made it a special target when they attacked a group of young protest marchers. In Paris, gendarmes took special pains to barber prisoners whose hair length they found offensive. In South Korea, police rounded up youths with long hair and cut it off. In Singapore, authorities refused to admit to the country a traveling American journalist until he had his hair trimmed at the airport.

As the reaction to long hair suggests, virtually any characteristic may be interpreted as deviant, from an attitude to a physical attribute. In fact, one series of experiments suggests that the mere appearance of being different is enough to arouse group aggression—even if the difference does not really mean anything. In 1968 at Stanford University, psychologists Jonathan Freedman and Anthony Doob contrived a way to create meaningless deviance. Working with groups of five or six subjects, they gave each person a battery of written personality tests. After a while, each subject was shown score sheets that were purported to contain the results of the test for all the members of his group.

These sheets did not show actual scores for each person but only the relative distribution of scores among the group—for example, Person A in the middle of the scale, Person B at the high end and so on. The results were phony—they had been prepared long before the subjects took the tests. They were rigged so that one member of the group was given a score that put him at the high or low end of the scale. He would be the extreme deviant. Two others were given scores that made them seem slightly deviant. The remaining members of the group were assigned scores at the middle of the scale. For the purposes of the experiment, those subjects would be nondeviant.

The experimenters then assessed their subjects' newly created feelings of deviancy or nondeviancy. They asked the subjects to answer questions such as "How different do you feel from most people of your age and sex?" by rating themselves on a scale that ranged from "very similar" to "extremely different." Subjects were also asked to rate others in the group. The results confirmed that the ruse had been successful. Only one member of the group felt truly deviant—though he did not know precisely how he was different from the others—and the rest of the group also regarded him as different. He was, of course, the subject assigned the extreme score in the prepared result sheet.

The group was then asked to select one of its members for a sup-

The incendiary appeals of wartime

"WANTS YOU"

As every revolutionary knows, one of the most effective ways to arouse the citizenry to violence is with posters. Their message is simple, and their impact is sharp. They employ a bold visual image, usually accompanied by a slogan that is brief and hard-hitting, to urge the viewer to fight.

Posters incite group aggression by varied appeals to the emotions. There is the rallying call to the flag that impels violence in the name of patriotism; and there are the posters that degrade the enemy by depicting him as a monster that can ethically be destroyed. Still others appeal to fear, by symbolizing the enemy as a threatening aggressor.

Some poster images are so powerful that they are repeated in different nations: the compelling design of the poster at left was imitated by American artist James Montgomery Flagg, who showed Uncle Sam in an identical pose in a famous "I Want You" poster, of which more than four million copies were distributed during World War I.

Obedience to authority, a potent motive for wartime aggression, is summoned by this British recruiting poster of World War I employing a painting of the famed Army Field Marshal and Secretary for War, Lord Herbert Kitchener. He points imperiously at the viewer, commanding him to join Britain's military forces.

Dehumanizing the enemy—in order to make the act of killing him no more repellent than the destruction of an animal—is a favorite propaganda device. This German World War II poster represents Soviet forces as a many-headed serpent that must be stabbed to death by patriotic, flag-wielding soldiers.

In an appeal to the humanitarian impulse
to protect the helpless, this poster shows
a mother and child being menaced by
bombers and asks, "What will you do to
stop this?" It was distributed in France
in the 1930s by Spanish Republicans who
hoped to enlist Frenchmen in their
cause during the Civil War in Spain.

posedly painful task—a learning experiment that purportedly would require him to receive electric shocks. The nondeviants singled out the extreme deviant as the target even though they had no idea how he differed from the rest of the group. By the same token, the extreme deviant skipped over the slightly deviant members and chose only nondeviants for the punishment—just as real-life dissenters often tend to reciprocate the group's aggression against them.

Deviance is a kind of psychological twin to another potential cause of group aggression: prejudice. Both involve perceptions of differences in people, but the hostility of prejudice is directed at people outside the group rather than at dropouts from the group. And the differences that give rise to prejudice tend to be more deeply rooted in race, religion and ethnic background.

Prejudice can be defined as an attitude that legitimizes the selection of people outside the group as victims of aggression or discrimination, but it is not always a foolproof predictor of overt behavior. For people do not always practice what they preach, especially in the realm of discrimination, and sometimes this truism can take an unexpected turn. A classic experiment demonstrated this point in 1933, when prejudice against Orientals was prevalent in the United States and such antidiscrimination laws as existed were not enforced. A white psychologist, R. T. LaPiere, and a well-dressed Chinese couple traveled across the country quietly testing anti-Oriental biases. They sought lodging and meals in 67 hotels and motels and 184 restaurants. They were turned away only once, although the refusal of service on racial grounds was common at the time.

Six months later LaPiere sent a letter to the same establishments asking if the managers would accept Chinese guests. Only one of the 251 managers answered in the affirmative—and that in a chatty letter describing the nice visit the manager had enjoyed with a Chinese gentleman and his wife some six months before. This gaping inconsistency between professed bigotry and actual behavior suggests two conclusions. First, people do not always act on their prejudices. And the external pressures of a situation—a respectable-looking couple asking for food or rooms—can override the deepest-rooted inner feelings of hostility.

What causes prejudice is not clear. What is clear is its role in causing violence. Prejudice most often leads to aggression when a group is frustrated in achieving its aims. Members are then likely to displace their aggressive feelings onto scapegoats from other racial, ethnic or religious groups. This process was studied in research at a camp for young unemployed men in the late 1930s. The experiment took place on a Friday night, when the young men of the isolated camp were supposed to attend a movie in a nearby town, an occasion eagerly awaited because money was to be given away at the theater. The youths were asked to indicate on questionnaires their feelings about two minority groups, Americans of Japanese and Mexican descent. Then the experimenters deliberately frustrated their subjects by giving them a series of difficult tests. The tests took so long to complete that it soon became clear to the subjects they would be deprived of their long-awaited trip to the movie. After the tests, the subjects were again asked to indicate their feelings about Japanese- and Mexican-Americans. The youths, now frustrated and angry, vented their displeasure by recording far fewer favorable comments about the minority groups.

Their targets represented ideal scapegoats. They were visibly different in their appearance and language and—unlike the high-status experimenters who caused the frustration—relatively safe targets for aggression. Above all, they were already disliked by many of the subjects. This factor, other experiments suggest, increases the likelihood of aggression. For example, a group of college students known to be anti-Semitic were subjected to frustration, then asked to write stories based upon pictures they were shown. When the experimenters gave Jewish-sounding names to the characters in the pictures, the subjects directed far more aggression toward them in their stories.

Once prejudice is instilled in a group, conformity helps perpetuate it. A study of racial tension in South Africa, for example, showed that those who were bigoted against blacks also were more likely to conform to a variety of other social norms. And other studies, in the United States, suggest that some people may feel racial prejudice simply out of conformity to local custom. In these studies, whites who lived in Southern towns where antiblack feeling ran high generally expressed prejudiced attitudes. But if they moved to a more liberal geographical area, they then tended to conform to new group norms and professed far less prejudice against blacks.

One widespread cause of group frustration is economic or political competition for limited resources. If jobs, land or other sources of wealth are scarce, one group is likely to lose out. In fact, some instances of what appeared to be religious warfare in the 1970s —Protestants versus Catholics in Northern Ireland *(pages 132-143)* or Christians versus Moslems in Lebanon—may be better accounted for in terms of the frustrations arising from the competition for resources. In England, prejudice against blacks did not become apparent until immigrants from the former colonies began moving into industrial cities and competing for jobs. And Yale psychologist John Dollard, in a famous study of social relationships in a small American town, described how aggression against German immigrants increased as jobs became scarce, even though the townspeople had previously shown no pattern of prejudice against Germans.

Demagogues all over the world have long known the malevolent value of whipping up group hatreds, frustrations and prejudices to arouse their followers to aggression. The master, of course, was Adolf Hitler. Faced with the frustration and economic chaos of Germany early in the 1930s, he took advantage of endemic anti-Semitism, and lashed it with fiendish skill. He made workers feel that Jewish capitalists were to blame for German economic problems and he made the industrialists feel that Jewish labor agitators were at fault. And with his offer of a simple and terrible "solution," a *judenfrei* Germany, he united the people and prepared them to become agents in the systematic destruction of six million human beings.

In carrying out his effort to eliminate the Jews, Hitler made use of a potent technique for inciting one group to aggression against another: dehumanizing the victims. Most human beings are unwilling to bring pain to another human. This inhibition can be reduced if the victim is perceived as nonhuman: an object or an animal. This fact is well known to surgeons, who receive special training in overcoming their reluctance to cut into a human being. They are taught to perceive the patient on the table as a body, not a person. Hitler began to dehumanize Jews by excluding them from status as citizens and finally denied them status as human beings. Survivors of the death camps testified that the Jews were treated—and themselves came to feel—as if they were less than human. Like animals, they were forced to go unclothed, they were tattooed with identifying numbers and sprayed with insecticide, and they were transported on cattle trains. The dehumanization made them easier for the Nazis to "exterminate."

The Nazis had no monopoly on the use of dehumanization to justify group violence. It is a universal practice. During World War I the British government issued posters caricaturing German soldiers as pigs. The lexicon of abusive labels applied by nations to their enemies pungently emphasizes an identification with animals: rats, swine, imperialist running dogs.

Americans have added to the vocabulary of aggression at home and abroad. At home violence has been directed at "niggers," "honkies," "wops" and "kikes"—all applications that separate targets of preju-

Accused of stabbing a crippled youth in a park in Manhattan, members of a gang called the Egyptian Kings are arraigned for murder.

The problem of the street gang

Among the more senseless forms of violence are the periodic outbreaks of killing and maiming that are committed by young street gangs. The youths, suddenly materializing on an urban street, stage swift, unprovoked attacks. Since they may strike total strangers as well as members of rival gangs, they often terrorize an entire community.

A four-year study of New York City street gangs by criminologist Lewis Yablonsky found that the violent ones consist of a cadre of leaders and their close followers, surrounded by youngsters who may drift in and out of the gang without participating in the violence. Unlike these marginal members, the gang's core youths suffer from severe emotional disturbances. Raised in slums, often by absentee parents who

are away all day working, and frequently the victims of racial prejudice, they are filled with resentment that is vented in various acts of violence.

By coming together in a gang, Yablonsky reported, these youths seek to give legitimacy to their violent behavior and avoid being considered insane, as might happen if they were to act alone. This conclusion was supported by research done in Glasgow, Scotland, which found members of that city's notorious gangs haunted by a morbid fear they might actually be mentally ill. Gang members' submergence of their individual pathology in group violence succeeds, according to Yablonsky, because society, though officially disapproving, is covertly intrigued with the gangs and tends to glorify them.

dice from ordinary humanity. In Vietnam, American soldiers felt they were killing "dinks," "slopes" or "gooks." The sum of the enemy dead was no more than a "body count." Considering this attitude, it is small wonder perhaps that before Lieutenant William Calley went on trial for the massacre at My Lai, his psychiatric report said: "He did not feel as if he were killing humans, but rather that they were animals with whom one could not speak or reason."

Even pejorative stereotypes serve as a kind of dehumanization, making victims more susceptible to aggression. The British found it easier to kill Germans if they were Huns (after the Asian barbarians who devastated Europe in the Fifth Century under Attila). The French preferred the label Boche (literally, German blockhead). Nazi-era films, in keeping with Hitler's Aryan racial ideology, cast their heroes as big, blond and blue-eyed and the villains as small, dark-haired and dark-eyed.

Experiments conducted recently in West Germany, some three decades after the fall of the Third Reich, suggest that such stereotypes had remarkable staying power but could be changed by the same medium that first instilled them. The subjects were invited to a Cologne television studio, ostensibly to preview some new movies. They were shown slides of actors who conformed to one or the other of the old stereotypes. When they were asked to evaluate the actors in terms of personality and suitable roles, it was clear the old stereotypes had survived. The dark actors were seen as significantly slier, wickeder and more amoral, and suitable for villainous roles such as swindlers and pimps. However, the subjects' views changed substantially when they were shown a number of TV movies in which the stereotypes were reversed—with the dark actors playing the good guys for a change. And when the original experiment was conducted using younger Germans, students who had not been exposed to Nazi propaganda, there was much less evidence of adherence to the old blond-dark stereotypes.

By dehumanizing the enemy, a group and its members justify to themselves their aggression against him. Interestingly, this tendency often persists even after a victim has suffered injury or death. The group not only continues to perceive him as less than human but transfers the blame to the victim himself, who frequently is said to have "got what was coming to him."

A remarkable example of this effect occurred in 1970 after the tragic confrontation between soldiers and student antiwar protesters at Kent State University in Ohio. Four students were shot to death. Two of the victims were innocent bystanders not involved in the demonstration. In a poll taken shortly afterward, 60 per cent of the people who were questioned blamed the demonstrating students for the deaths. Only 11 per cent blamed the soldiers who had opened fire. The majority sentiments were echoed by President Richard Nixon, who suggested that the demonstrators had invited the tragedy.

The blame-the-victim syndrome was even stronger among the townspeople of Kent—most of whom felt themselves allied with the soldiers in a loose-knit group that stood for law and order. Rumors spread quickly about the four victims, all of whom had been worthy, upright young men and women. One rumor had it that their corpses were filthy, lice-ridden and so riddled with syphilis that the students would have died in two weeks anyway. One schoolteacher spoke for many townspeople when she said flatly: "Anyone who appears on the streets of a city like Kent with long hair, dirty clothes or barefooted deserves to be shot."

One explanation for such post-mortem derogation of the victims is the psychological need of the townspeople to preserve their positive image of themselves and of their larger law-abiding group—those who subscribed to status-quo respectability. The mental process involved is what psychologists call "cognitive dissonance," and it occurs when a person has two ideas or attitudes that are inconsistent with each other. In Kent the townspeople's notion that "we're nice people" clashed with the fact that the legitimate representatives of their group, the soldiers, had killed innocent students. By devaluing the victims, the townspeople could protect their own self-esteem and justify what might have seemed to them to be inconsistent behavior.

This explanation was tested by psychologists Melvin Lerner and Carolyn Simmons in a University of Kentucky laboratory experiment. Their subjects watched for 10 minutes while an accomplice of the experimenter appeared to suffer electric shocks. If the subjects were given the opportunity to stop the suffering, they showed little inclination afterward to derogate the victim. But if, like the people of Kent, who had no real control over the actions of the soldiers, they were powerless to stop it, they rejected and devalued her.

"For their own security, if for no other reason, people want to believe they live in a just world where people get what they deserve," explained Lerner. "Any evidence of undeserved suffering threatens this belief. The observer then will attempt to reestablish justice. One way of accomplishing this is by acting to compensate the victim; another is persuading himself that the victim deserved to suffer."

That is the great paradox of group violence. People rationalize acts of aggression and blame the victim of the acts rather than the aggressor.

When violence breeds violence

"Violence almost never ends simply with a rectification of the conditions that brought it about," reported social psychologist Elliot Aronson. "Violence breeds violence." That grim result is all the more likely when groups are involved. For people will do things in groups that they would never do on their own. Groups set standards of behavior for their members and provide pressures to make them conform. And when violence has erupted, the involvement of large numbers of people greatly increases the likelihood that it will spread with unstoppable momentum.

All these elements quickly became apparent in the catastrophic fighting that broke out in Northern Ireland in 1968.

This tiny enclave had been born out of violence in 1923 when the southern part of the island won its independence from England, and the six counties of Northern Ireland opted to stay under British rule. Sixty per cent of the 1.5 million population were Protestants, descendants of British settlers who had emigrated in 1602. Fiercely loyal to England, they rejected union with the rest of Ireland. The other 40 per cent were Roman Catholics of indigenous stock, who did not accept the 1923 partition of Ireland as permanent. Both sides maintained clandestine paramilitary forces—a scattering of Protestant groups dedicated to the status quo, and aggressive units of the Irish Republican Army devoted to unification of the island under Catholic rule.

As a result of this splitting of the country into hostile groups, violence found a congenial environment when it broke out. It fed on itself and grew, at terrible cost.

Charging to put down an outbreak of stoning in the city of Londonderry's Catholic ghetto, a phalanx of British soldiers carrying plastic shields, truncheons and machine guns rushes past women cowering in their doorways. The soldiers were dispatched to Ireland to put down violence, but they came to be considered protectors by the Protestants and agents of oppression by the Catholics.

The division in Northern Ireland's society is starkly evident in Londonderry. Bogside (near right), the low-lying depressed Catholic section, is separated from the Protestant residential area to the far right by the old town wall. The cannon (foreground) was used to defend the city against Catholic siege in 1690.

Haves pitted against have-nots

From the time Northern Ireland became a British colony, a potential for group violence existed there because of the widespread prejudice between Protestant and Catholic. Though prejudice does not always erupt in violence, a study directed by social psychologist Muzafer Sherif showed how it can.

Sherif divided boys in an American summer camp into two groups and pitted them against each other in highly competitive games. In no time, hostility between the groups sprang up; when one received special treatment at a party, a riot ensued. Sherif's conclusion: competition between groups breeds a virulent prejudice that a precipitating incident may cause to explode.

In Northern Ireland, the competition was for a decent living in a depressed economy; Catholics lost out because they were discriminated against. When a reform government finally did make some concessions to the Catholics, their expectations were raised. They were encouraged to demonstrate against discrimination, and their protests in turn inspired a backlash from the Protestants—which brought on violence.

The Coyles, a Catholic family of Bogside, gather for a frugal tea (left). Forced by discrimination to live in poor, cramped quarters like these, Catholics were also gerrymandered out of the political power they needed to fight for better housing.

In the opposite camp, a British Union Jack is hoisted by a Protestant woman and her grandson (partially visible at the far right) before their tidy Belfast cottage. Protestants often complained that Catholics were not as neat as they. Said one housewife, "Why can't they fix up their houses like decent people do?"

The bloody point of no return

In August 1969, amid heightened tension that was brought on by the increasing number of Roman Catholic civil rights demonstrations, Londonderry Protestants staged their annual march through the city in celebration of a 1690 defeat of Catholic forces. As the marchers reached the outskirts of the Bogside Catholic ghetto, a Bogsider fired a marble from a slingshot at them. His act was one that sociologists have called a "key stimulus," because it acted, like a key opening a lock, to remove inhibitions that previously prevented the release of aggression.

Within moments Bogside erupted in violence. When British soldiers were brought in to quell this uprising, and the I.R.A. mobilized for action, the stage was set for further violence.

Running for cover, a British soldier is felled by a stone hurled by a Catholic in Londonderry's Bogside during the five-day 1969 riot. The crowd cheered and concentrated its attack on him until his companions dragged him to safety.

Four years later, in a drastic escalation of violence, a Catholic man lies dying on a Bogside street, shot by British troops during a run-in with participants in a prohibited civil rights march. The disaster, which became known as Bloody Sunday, left 13 Catholics dead and brought a vow of revenge from the I.R.A.

Masked recruits of the Irish Republican Army, teen-age girls learn to load a machine gun in training at Londonderry. The masks hiding their faces, like the helmets, dark glasses and jackets of the Protestant fighters opposite, also blur their sense of personal identity, and make them more willing to act violently.

Mobilizing for full-scale war

The Bloody Sunday killings further polarized Northern Ireland by inflaming the Catholics and increasing the influence and activities of I.R.A. terrorists. This in turn brought cries for repression of the I.R.A. from the Protestants, who augmented their units with a new military organization called the Ulster Defense Association, or U.D.A. Both sides then moved toward greater violence by enlisting more troops.

The tactic was not new, for revolutionaries from Lenin to Mao Tse-tung have recognized the value of organiz-

ing people into formal military units in order to exploit their potential for violence. Psychologists explain the effectiveness of this move as a result of "deindividuation": the submerging of the individual into the group. They cite studies showing that group membership reduces individual restraints and makes people more prone to aggression by blurring their identities. In line with this finding, the anonymity of identically uniformed soldiers makes it easier for them to commit the acts of violence that warfare makes legitimate.

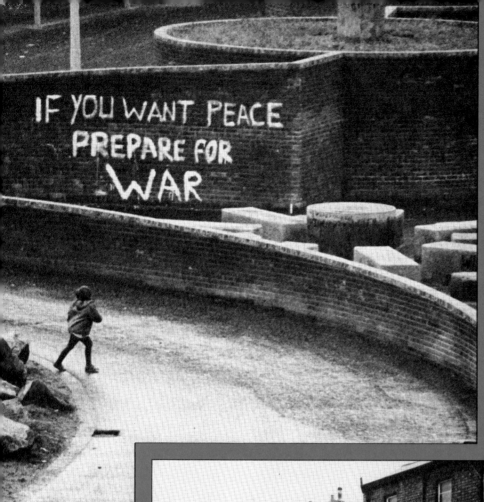

An ominous forecast of the rapidly deteriorating situation in Northern Ireland is scrawled on a wall in Divis Flats, a Belfast Catholic district.

Standing guard at the entrance to Shankill, a Protestant district of Belfast, these members of the Ulster Defense Association, which was established in 1972, flank a homemade street barrier.

Suffering, bitterness, fury

Though the casualty rate in Northern Ireland was high—more than 1,300 dead and almost 13,000 injured in the first six years of open conflict—the suffering did not deter violence but intensified it. Experts explain this paradox with the "dissonance" theory of psychologist Leon Festinger.

According to Festinger, dissonance is a gap between an individual's beliefs and his behavior. Most people try to close this gap by bringing either their beliefs or their behavior into conformity. In Northern Ireland, it was beliefs. Heavy casualties caused both Catholics and Protestants to believe more deeply in their causes—precipitating more violence and still heavier casualties.

The widow of a victim of Bloody Sunday weeps inconsolably at her husband's funeral. Such experiences steeled many women to engage in violence themselves. Said one, "Before women had just silently suffered. Now they go out to protest. If the soldiers fire gas at them, it makes them more determined."

A terrible legacy for the young

Perhaps the most tragic victims of the fighting in Northern Ireland were the children. Substantiating a 1963 study, which found that youngsters learn aggression by seeing aggression in those they admire, they quickly emulated the exploits of the much-praised I.R.A. or U.D.A. fighters. Hurling gas bombs at the age of eight, some became machine-gun-toting guerrillas by 15. Psychologists said they would be changed for life by their experience. For the lesson they have learned is that violence is an acceptable solution to human problems.

Staging what is known as "the daily 5 o'clock riot on William Street," boys in Londonderry throw stones at a British Army van as it approaches on its rounds. In some areas, such youngsters presented the most serious danger the soldiers faced.

Boys in a Belfast alley remain amused and derisive while a British soldier frisks them for weapons. Yet the search was grimly necessary: such boys would sometimes carry—and use—loaded guns.

Muzzling the Menace

"I was shocked at your advice to the mother whose three-year-old had temper tantrums," begins a letter to the popular American newspaper columnist Ann Landers. "You suggested that the child be taught to kick the furniture and 'get the anger out of his system.' I always thought you were a little cuckoo. Now I'm sure. My younger brother used to kick the furniture when he got mad. Mother called it 'letting off steam.' Well, he's 32 years old now and still kicking the furniture—what's left of it, that is. He is also kicking his wife, the cat, the kids, and anything else that gets in his way. Last October he threw the TV set out of the window when his favorite team failed to score and lost the game. (The window was closed at the time.) Why don't you tell mothers that children must be taught to control their anger? This is what separates civilized human beings from savages, Dummy."

More succinctly than any scientist—and certainly more colorfully —the reader summed up two major ideas about how to deal with aggression. The first view, prevalent not only among newspaper columnists but among many scientists as well, holds that aggressive feelings build up like steam in a boiler, and they must be provided with outlets. The other approach, growing out of an impressive body of experimental research, proposes that aggression can be controlled through learning and through manipulation of situations that generate aggression—in the way the youthful protester at left tries to mollify threatening soldiers by placing carnations in the muzzles of their rifles.

The first approach is known as the catharsis theory and owes its popularity to the writings of Sigmund Freud. Freud believed that the expression of aggressive feelings has a cathartic value—that a person feels better afterward and in addition his tendency to violence is temporarily reduced. Catharsis fits neatly with the theories of those who believe, as Freud did, that man is inherently aggressive. But it also has been endorsed by many psychologists who hold that aggression is learned, stemming from such environmental factors as frustration. In either view the steam builds up and has to be released—through an aggressive act or through socially accepted outlets.

The purported outlets for aggressive energy cover a remarkable range of human activity. One is violence itself—a physical or verbal attack. Physical work and even creative effort have been held to lessen aggression. And participation in, or vicarious enjoyment of, violent play is widely held to release aggression under conditions that prevent serious harm.

There is much historical and anthropological support for these ideas, for behavior of the type that is supposed to aid catharsis can be perceived in many societies, ancient and modern, the world over. It is evident in some cultures that are notably nonviolent. This behavior is institutionalized in rituals that suspend the normal prohibitions against antisocial acts, but under rules limiting the danger *(pages 32-41)*. Some rituals permit the release of only verbal aggression. In India the spring festival of Holi allows citizens to insult public figures with impunity; Eskimos—who eschew almost all physical violence—periodically gather to exchange songs of outrageous personal abuse. Physical violence is even more widely ritualized—the competitive sports of industrialized nations are seen by some as parallels to the ritualized combat between male deer or the sham warfare of such tribes as the Kurelu of New Guinea, who engage the enemy just beyond arrow range, a tactic that permits them to fight fiercely while seldom hitting anyone.

Such socially sanctioned outlets for aggression must serve some purpose or they would not have lasted so long in so many diverse societies. This purpose has been assumed to be catharsis, but a growing body of evidence now questions the cathartic effects of certain behavior, suggesting that whatever ritualized aggression accomplishes, it does not reduce aggressive tension and make people more peaceful.

In recent years psychologists have tested the catharsis theory in controlled laboratory experiments. Like many of Freud's brilliant intuitions, catharsis contains a kernel of truth surrounded by misleading oversimplifications. In experiments catharsis sometimes occurs, but only under highly specific circumstances. The effect depends upon the nature of the aggression (for example, whether verbal or physical), whom it is directed against and the emotional state of the aggressor.

The complex influences that help or hinder the working out of aggressiveness were revealed by investigation of the notion that committing aggression makes a person feel better by reducing tension. Psychologist Jack E. Hokanson of Florida State University staged experiments in which anger and tension were directly measured by physiological stress indicators such as blood pressure and heart rate. First, Hokanson's subjects were aroused by being insulted. Then the subjects were allowed to retaliate by delivering fake shocks to the person who had angered them. The results were dramatic: in less than one minute, blood pressure and other indicators of stress returned to preinsult levels.

Such effects were achieved only when the subject was angry and when his aggression was directed at the source of his anger. In a variation of the experiment, Hokanson provided several different targets for his angered subjects. One was introduced to the subjects as the experimenter. Another was introduced as the experimenter's assistant, a third as a psychology student and a fourth as just another student. Hokanson found that the more remote the target's relationship to the original source of anger—the experimenter—the less the cathartic effect. In fact, retaliating against a target who was introduced as just another student produced no tension reduction at all.

Hokanson's results suggest that in real life a child angered by his father may get some physiological relief from hurting his big sister but little or none from hitting the boy down the street. But Hokanson focused on physiological measures of stress, which may reflect not only aggressiveness but also other kinds of emotional arousal, such as fear, elation or even just excitement. When different measures of aggressiveness are used—for example, the subject's report of his feelings or the experimenter's evaluation of them—the cathartic effect of retaliation seems partly to confirm Hokanson's results but also to differ from them in critical aspects. For one thing, while hurting big sister or the boy down the street may not reduce physiological stress, it may alleviate feelings of aggressiveness and reduce the potential for further violence.

These possibilities are raised by a series of experiments conducted at the University of Toronto by Anthony Doob. His work shows that if the aggressor is already angry, the expression of his anger in violence will temporarily reduce his aggressiveness. What is more, Doob found the same aggression-reducing effect when the subject did not administer the punishment but merely watched his tormentor suffer.

One explanation of these results is that people who hurt the tormentor or watch him suffer feel the score has been evened. But another experiment by Vladimir Konečni and Doob suggests otherwise. Subjects were angered and some were made to believe they had the chance to shock a scapegoat—an innocent stranger who was not associated in any way with their tormentor. Later, they were also given a chance to even the score by hurting the person who had angered them. They proved to

be far less aggressive to their tormentor than those who had not been given a chance to hurt the innocent stranger. Apparently they had got rid of much of their aggression by displacing it onto the scapegoat.

In demonstrating that physical violence against an enemy or a scapegoat releases and reduces aggression, such experiments support some traditional beliefs about the value of catharsis as a regulator of violence. But their support is sharply limited. Other beliefs about catharsis, equally widespread, have been disproved.

The conditions of the Doob and Hokanson studies rarely exist in everyday life; a person seldom can take physical action against the source of his anger. He is much more likely to resort to verbal assault. Many people believe that saying bad things to or about a tormentor is effective catharsis, draining off aggressive feelings and leaving the speaker less hostile. The laboratory evidence, however, indicates that verbal aggression does not reduce hostility. Some experiments, in fact, suggest that a verbal assault has the opposite effect and increases aggressive feelings.

The most convincing demonstration of the way verbal aggression arouses emotions came from an experiment involving the real-life grievances of discharged workers. They had been among a group of several hundred engineers and technicians recruited by a company when it won a lucrative new contract. Less than a year later, the contract was abruptly canceled and about 200 of the new workers were fired.

At this point psychologist Ebbe B. Ebbesen and his colleagues from the University of California at San Diego undertook their unique study in catharsis. Their subjects were the workers who had been given layoff notices; unlike the subjects of laboratory experiments, they already had plenty to be disgruntled about. When hired, they had been promised a minimum of three years of work. Moreover, some 80 per cent of them had been laid off at least once before in their careers, many by the very same company. And to make matters worse, they learned of the impending layoff from newspaper accounts rather than their employer.

Ebbesen and his colleagues selected as subjects 100 of these workers. As their control group, they chose 48 engineers and technicians who were leaving the plant under happier circumstances, such as retirement, leaves of absence or transfers to other divisions, and thus were not likely to be angry. One of the experimenters installed himself in the personnel office, where, passing as a company staff member, he conducted "exit interviews" with each of the subjects.

The first few minutes of each interview consisted of a routine discussion of employee benefits and the subject's future plans. The

Venting his aggression, a Welsh youngster prepares to drop a rock on an already battered piano as playmates watch critically. Students of human behavior from Aristotle to Freud have held that diverting violence to inanimate objects purges aggressive impulses— but recent experiments do not affirm this.

149

remaining 20 minutes were carefully rigged. With one group of subjects the experimenter steered away from hostile comments about the company. But another group was encouraged to talk freely about anger against the company. And members of a third group were encouraged to air hostility toward their immediate supervisor at the plant. In both the second and third groups, leading questions about the fairness of the company or the supervisor made the laid-off workers get angrier as they talked. Some of them spilled out four-letter expletives of the kind seldom heard in laboratory experiments.

After each interview, the subject filled out various exit forms. These forms included questionnaires aimed at measuring the subject's verbal hostility toward the company or his supervisor. By the catharsis theory, a subject who had freely expressed his hostility during the interview a few minutes earlier should have got it off his chest. On the contrary, from the questionnaire replies, talking about it only seemed to have heightened the subjects' hostility toward supervisor or company.

These results are confirmed by a number of laboratory studies. In one experiment at Harvard, Michael Kahn—then a firm believer in the catharsis theory—told two groups of student subjects they were taking part in a medical experiment that required blood pressure and other physiological readings. Then both groups were insulted and humiliated by a technician, who took the readings while making slighting remarks about the subjects and extremely vulgar references to their families.

Next another experimenter, under the guise of physician in charge of the experiment, got one group of subjects to vent their anger about the technician's insulting behavior. The second group, who also had been insulted by the technician, were not given a chance to express their anger to the "physician." This group, by the catharsis theory, should have been tense and more aggressive. But the results were just the opposite: subjects who let off steam to the physician were even more hostile toward their tormentor than those who could not discuss their anger.

Why verbal aggression increases anger, and physical aggression may decrease it, is not clear. Perhaps dwelling on anger serves as self-arousal, just as rubbing a sore makes it hurt more. Then, too, verbal aggression does little to even the score; it is less likely than physical punishment to hurt the source or remove him as a future threat.

Whatever the reason for the differing effects, the findings about verbal aggression raise questions about the value of some methods of psychotherapy that have become increasingly popular in recent years. In these "ventilative therapies," patients are urged to ventilate bottled-up rage. To release pent-up aggressive energy, wrote psychiatrist

Alexander Lowen, "A woman subject is given a tennis racket and directed to beat the bed. While doing this she is asked to make an appropriate verbal statement such as 'I hate you,' 'I'll kill you.' The group, observing the subject's actions," added Lowen, "encourages her to be more aggressive, to let go, to let it out."

While these procedures may make some people feel better, University of Wisconsin psychologist Leonard Berkowitz charged that they also may render people more aggressive in the long run. Such techniques teach aggression by the effective processes of imitation and reward. The praise and encouragement of a therapy group, Berkowitz points out, reward make-believe aggression. This reinforcement might actually increase the chances of aggression afterward, outside the therapy situation. Experiments with children who were rewarded for attacking a large plastic doll *(Chapter 2)* showed they were more aggressive in later play. In another experiment, college students were rewarded just for uttering words with aggressive connotations; they proved far more willing to deliver electric shocks to fellow students than did subjects who were rewarded for neutral or helpful words.

Probably the most often used of all the purported cathartic outlets for aggression is intense physical activity, in work or play. Many a man has sought release from anger by chopping wood or going for a long walk, and many a woman has tried to dispel aroused emotions with a flurry of house cleaning. The calming influence of strenuous exercise is widely assumed to be more effective if the activity itself involves aggression or competition—the ritualized violence of modern sports and many ancient ceremonies. Neither idea stands up to close scrutiny.

Several experiments have assessed the value of pure physical activity, in which the exercise that was supposed to relieve aggressiveness did not involve violence. In one study, angered subjects who pounded nails into a board for 10 minutes were just as aggressive afterward. In a more elaborate experiment, one group of subjects gave real but mild electric shocks to another group of subjects to arouse them; the aroused subjects were then put through strenuous bouts on a stationary bicycle exerciser. The exercise not only failed to work off their anger, it seemed to increase their willingness, in a rigged part of the test, to deliver fake electric shocks to their original tormentors.

When violence is added to exercise, in contact sports such as football or hockey, the game seems to arouse the players even more than exercise alone. One factor is the element of competition: the losers almost always feel frustrated. Professional hockey has become so violent in recent years that authorities in Canada and the United States have brought criminal assault charges for incidents on the ice.

What about the cathartic value of merely viewing athletic contests —a practice long promoted as a harmless way of letting off steam vicariously? Disagreement over this aspect of the catharsis theory goes back to ancient times. Watching Greek tragedies, the philosopher Aristotle said, enabled spectators to purge their own emotions vicariously. Plato, on the other hand, said it would "arouse violent emotions and stir men to all sorts of passions."

Plato has been proved right—by observation of spectator conduct and by deliberate experiments. In Czechoslovakia, spectators celebrated a hockey victory over the Russians by ransacking the offices of the Soviet airline. In the United States, rioting broke out at a school basketball game and nine fans were stabbed. In Peru a ruling by a referee in a soccer match between a home team and one from Argentina set off rioting that ended in the deaths of over 300 persons. And riots after a soccer match between El Salvador and Honduras in 1969 were blamed for the severing of diplomatic relations between the two countries.

Ironically, spectator violence is unusually virulent in England, a nation not usually noted for unruliness. In recent seasons soccer hooliganism *(pages 97-99)* has been responsible for hundreds of personal asssaults each week, including pitched battles with the police. That the cause of the outbreaks is attendance at the game rather than any personality characteristic of people in the audience is indicated by one analysis. It found that while the typical soccer hooligan might be young and a heavy drinker, the spectator violence includes all kinds of people. "We have good evidence that many middle-aged, quiet and industrious men who are models of respectability at home and at work undergo a temporary personality transformation on Saturday afternoons and swear, shout and boo, and argue with the spectators nearby."

The psychological mechanisms at work in spectator behavior appear to be the same ones implicated in experiments involving the effects of viewing television and motion picture violence. Aggressive, no-holds-barred action on the field provides models for the fans to imitate. This modeling effect, one laboratory experiment shows, is enhanced if spectators think the players are out for blood and are not merely cool professionals unemotionally engaged in their business. The stronger the fan's feeling of identification with his favorite team, the greater the chance he will imitate player aggressiveness. Many British soccer fans intensify team identification, carrying scarves in team colors, shouting special chants and speaking an argot meaninglesss to outsiders.

continued on page 156

On the deck of a rescue boat, two teenagers learn to work with others as they help tow a disabled vessel. They were among 614 delinquents rehabilitated at the Florida Ocean Sciences Institute, where aggressive habits were redirected with behavior modification techniques in the guise of seamanship training.

Rechanneling aggression

At what looks like a seafaring camp for sons of the rich on Florida's sun-washed coast, behavior-modification techniques proved they could reduce violence in young criminals. This taming of extreme aggression—in boys convicted of such crimes as assault and armed robbery—was achieved by the use of rewards to encourage cooperation while discouraging selfish disregard of the rights of others.

Not a conventional reformatory, the Florida Ocean Sciences Institute was set up to teach the boys scuba diving and seamanship, as well as conventional physics and mathematics, while involving them in such useful projects as building an artificial reef to attract fish

and restoring a square-rigged vessel. Robert Rosof, the Institute's president and founder, commented, "The sea is a gimmick, a vehicle to bring about behavior change."

To induce change, progress at each step was rewarded. Badges, commendations and certificates honored good work; each month the best student won a trophy; and successful completion of the six-to-nine-month course brought a one-week Caribbean cruise.

Of the 120 or so delinquents rehabilitated at the Institute annually, 70 per cent returned to school or jobs. Only 14 per cent were later rearrested —compared to a national recidivism rate for juveniles of 64 per cent.

Under the watchful eye of an instructor
(far right), four boys check one another's
equipment at poolside in a scuba-diving
class. While acquiring a skill that can
lead to a job, they also learned far more
important lessons in cooperation.

A boy wearing scuba-diving equipment
comes to a fellow student's rescue in a
lifesaving class. "When you go diving,
you're responsible for your buddy's life,"
one youth said. "Many of us," he added,
"no one had ever given responsibility to."

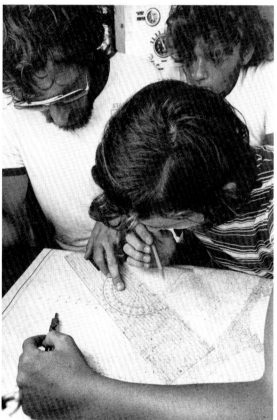

Earnestly leaning forward during a discussion session, three boys press a doubtful comrade (right) to stay with the program at FOSI. Impromptu meetings like this one were called whenever a member needed special encouragement, even if it meant interrupting a class.

A FOSI boy plots a course for a cruise to the Bahamas while his instructor and a fellow student watch. The trips, sought-after rewards for responsible behavior, were planned and executed by the boys.

President Robert Rosof (left) presents a trophy to the honor student of the month. Adept at winning group cooperation, this boy earned his award by helping to organize an underwater salvage project.

The excitement and color surrounding a big game also set the stage for anger and aggression. Studies conducted at athletic events in the United States show that subjects are more aggressive afterward—at least in part because of the size of the crowd, the loudness of the band and the chanting of the cheerleaders.

The aroused spectator may become even more aggressive if one of the players is injured, an experiment by psychologist Donald Hartmann at Stanford University indicates. He showed groups of boys several films portraying a basketball game between two youths. One film was essentially peaceful, another focused on indications of pain suffered by one player who was pummeled and kicked by the other, and the third showed the excited expressions of the aggressive player. After a group had seen one of these films, its members were tested by their willingness to administer what they thought would be real shocks. Those who had seen the film of the injured victim responded most aggressively.

Such studies demonstrate the sharply limited role that catharsis can play in countering aggression. Verbal assaults, kicking a football or watching a soccer game—none of these is likely to assuage an angry man. True, if he could physically attack the source of his anger, he might feel better and less aggressive, but then the source might counterattack and stir him up again.

What does work? Prevention and control, says the experimental evidence. Much of this research has centered on the environmental factors that arouse violence in the first place, especially frustration, and it suggests that many forms of aggression could be prevented by removing political and economic injustices that breed frustration, or by changing cultural values to turn people away from violence. Short of those utopian possibilities, a number of practical ways of alleviating everyday aggression have emerged from experiments. The research generally confirms common knowledge—but it reveals nuances in behavior that suggest why "what grandmother knew" works sometimes and not always. Two subtly different approaches have been discerned. One involves alterations in the conditions surrounding people so that they learn to avoid violence in expressing angry emotions. The second, more immediate approach identifies techniques that nullify anger before it can trigger aggression—allowing time for an aggressor to cool off, distracting him, offering recompense or explanations for the action that angered him, or appearing willing to accept his aggression in such a manner that he will be shamed into repressing it.

One of the simplest ways to cope with an enraged man, psychologists found, is just to let him cool off. Anger does subside, and if the angry man can be kept from violent action for 20 minutes to an hour, his aroused feelings are likely to evaporate.

The effect of time to cool off is indicated by a complex experiment at the University of Wisconsin by psychologists Mayra L. Buvinic and Leonard Berkowitz, using tests that depend on the known capacity of violent films to stimulate aggressiveness. The research team insulted male undergraduates, then showed them a particularly violent six-minute sequence of a boxing film. The experimenters let some subjects wait an hour before rating their aggressiveness from answers to a questionnaire. During that time their aggressive feelings cooled so markedly their test results showed little difference from those of a control group, which had been similarly insulted but had not been further aroused by viewing the movie. But cooling off could be prevented, Buvinic found, if aroused subjects were allowed to vent their aggression. Some subjects were tested immediately after the film and again an hour later. In their case the aggression-enhancing effect of the motion picture carried over. In effect, the practice in aggression afforded by the first test enabled their aroused aggressive tendencies to persist through the cooling-off period.

One way to help a person cool off is to distract him. At the University of Toronto, subjects were shown a filmed gun fight to arouse them. Then some were given a 15-minute routine eye examination to distract them. When both groups were tested for aggression—by their willingness to administer what they thought were electric shocks in a faked learning experiment—those who had undergone the eye examination were less willing to give shocks than the others. Presumably the examination reduced their arousal simply by taking their minds off it.

Although angry emotions dissipate fairly quickly, they may not do so quickly enough to avert aggression. An active countermove rather than a passive one may be called for. Among the most effective is the one animals use: appeasement *(Chapter 1)*. This acknowledgment of the aggressor's right to be aroused—of the propriety of his response to an offense against him—generally neutralizes anger and inhibits its expression in violent action.

Humans also employ rituals somewhat akin to appeasement gestures. They shake hands or offer a potential enemy a cigarette. Occasionally, more dramatic displays of appeasement are required; perhaps the most extreme—not to say outrageous—of recent years was the demand of the tyrannical President of Uganda, Idi Amin, that British envoys grovel on their knees to save a countryman from public execution.

Though Lorenz blamed human violence on a seeming lack of rituals

for conveying appeasement, man in fact possesses a uniquely effective means for communicating this idea to an angry member of his species: language. A few words—"I'm sorry" or "It won't happen again"—have cooled off more arguments than anyone can count.

With language, humans can go beyond animal-like appeasement in controlling aggression. Language provides unlimited resources for explaining precisely those actions that the potential adversary might otherwise take as an affront. Perhaps the most vivid illustration of the power of such exchanges in averting violence is the "hot line" that keeps Moscow and Washington in continuous contact, enabling leaders of the two powers to communicate with each other at any instant and thus prevent misunderstandings from escalating into nuclear war.

Many experiments show the formidable effect of a few words of explanation. If subjects who are deliberately aroused are told that their tormentor was handicapped in some way or did not mean to anger them, they tend to respond to his attacks and insults less aggressively. The timing of such an explanation is critical. In a study at the University of Indiana by Dolf Zillmann, some subjects were informed before being provoked that their tormentor was worried about a test he had to take. Others were told after he had insulted them. When both groups were given a chance to retaliate against the tormentor—by answering questions that supposedly would influence his chances for advancement —those who knew about the mitigating circumstances ahead of time were much less hostile than the others.

These differences in psychological reactions were confirmed by physiological reactions. Such indicators of arousal as blood pressure and heart rate were monitored throughout the experiment. They rose less among those subjects who had prior knowledge of the tormentor's problem—the explanation kept them from becoming very angry when he provoked them. Strangely, the blood pressure and heartbeat indicators of physiological arousal quickly returned to normal among the subjects who did not know of the mitigating circumstances until after being insulted, a result suggesting that their arousal did not last very long—but their psychological anger persisted. On the questionnaire they were just as hostile toward the tormentor as was the control group, which was never given any explanation of his problem. Apparently once a person makes up his mind to retaliate, this intention may persist even after physiological arousal subsides.

This experiment and others that measure the effect of mitigating circumstances dramatize the critical role of the mind in controlling aggression. Severe provocation does not have to trigger anger and aggression automatically. How a person responds depends on the way he thinks—on his interpretation of an event, on his motivation and on what he has been taught by previous experience. If the motivation is powerful enough, he can learn to respond peaceably to provocation that normally would be almost certain to trigger violence.

Some of the most convincing demonstrations of the ability to learn restraint in trying circumstances come from political actions applying doctrines of nonviolence developed by Mohandas K. Gandhi *(pages 166-167)*. Gandhi in India, and later Martin Luther King Jr. in the United States, achieved momentous social change by organizing people to upset the existing patterns of life—but always peaceably. Indian protesters disrupted train service by lying en masse across railroad tracks; American blacks violated segregation laws by sitting quietly in restaurant sections that were legally restricted to whites. Such actions took great courage because they were likely to incite violent retaliation from the police or even bystanders. They also required powerful self-control, for if the protesters were to succeed in their aim they had to remain peaceful in the face of violent retaliation. When black activists staged sit-ins at segregated lunch counters in the United States in the early 1960s, they were cursed, spat upon and physically brutalized. Yet the vast majority responded by turning the other cheek. They were able to do so partly because they were strongly motivated but also because some had learned nonviolence, rehearsing it in special workshops where for many hours they practiced passive resistance under simulated attack.

In less dramatic ways everyone learns to be nonaggressive in certain situations. The mechanisms are the same ones by which aggression itself is learned—repetition, reward, imitation of a model, punishment. Of these mechanisms, reward is generally considered the most effective one—the only effective one in the opinion of some psychologists.

The reward must be great to motivate the quick learning of such remarkable restraint as that displayed by the followers of Gandhi and King. In their case the reward was great: independence from colonialism, acceptance as first-class citizens. But simpler rewards consistently proffered over long periods of time have equal power, particularly in the teaching of children to develop nonaggressive behavior, and of these simple rewards, none is more potent than parental love.

Studies of many kinds are remarkably consistent in their findings that love-oriented techniques work best in the development of nonviolent behavior. Statistical research comparing families in several cultures showed that those cultures most effective in instilling permanent ethical values in their children were those that rewarded good behavior with affectionate praise and punished aggression only by holding back affection and approval. Among the Eskimos, for example, where fighting is almost unknown, children seem by Western standards to be spoiled. Affection is lavished on them. Their parents consistently reward them by praising them for "remembering" what they have been taught and seem never to charge them harshly with disobedience.

Further confirmation of the power of stressing constructive behavior comes from controlled experiments such as the one carried out by Joel Davitz at Teachers College, Columbia University. Davitz put small groups of children, aged seven to nine, through a series of competitive games. Some of the groups were praised for their aggressive responses during the games. Other groups were praised for any constructive and cooperative behavior they displayed.

Afterward, Davitz aroused angry emotions in all the groups by subjecting them to teeth-grinding frustration. He started to show them some entertaining movies and, after a few minutes, he further whetted their expectations by passing out candy bars. Just as the film reached a climax, he stopped it and took away the uneaten candy bars. Then he encouraged the children to play freely with toys such as small hammers and saws. Those who earlier had been praised for aggressive behavior used the hammers and saws to destroy things. The ones who had been rewarded for good behavior used the same kinds of toys to build things. They were less aggressive by comparison with the other children, and most were less aggressive than they had been before being trained to expect praise for constructive behavior.

Thus, constructive behavior can occur even after severe frustration if that behavior has been made appealing by prior training. Additional evidence comes from the experiments that have established a link between youthful aggression and watching violence on television. Positive programs, which emphasized cooperative behavior and self-discipline, tended to promote high levels of obedience to social rules, tolerance of delay and persistence at frustrating tasks.

Positive reinforcement for positive behavior is much more effective at restraining violence than is negative reinforcement for negative conduct—i.e., punishing misbehavior. Punishment can have the opposite effect, increasing rather than reducing violent tendencies—if the punishment itself is violent *(Chapter 2)*. But some types of punishment do seem to prevent aggression.

The threat of punishment can deter aggression among both children and adults, provided the threat is credible—if it is seen by potential aggressors as certain to be carried out for every offense. Most people, of course, are restrained from violence by the presence of a policeman. This effect can carry over when the enforcing authority is not on the scene but is believed nearby. One little-known example is the vivid contrast in lawlessness that characterized the 19th Century push westward in two neighboring countries, the United States and Canada. Virtually none of the fabled violence of the American West accompanied the settling of the Canadian Klondike. This anomaly has been attributed to the forceful presence of the North-West Mounted Police, who went west with the first settlers and enforced the laws. Even the spirit of a policeman can prevent violence. In Tahiti, the traditional religion casts ancestral spirits in the role of ever-present police. Children are taught that anger will arouse the spirits, who will then punish them with illness and injury. And Tahitian culture is remarkably free of aggression.

American psychologists, lacking spirits to evoke, have sought to determine why certain kinds of punishments and threats of punishment

are effective in influencing behavior. Some of the most interesting experiments did not directly involve aggression, but their results almost certainly apply to the process by which children learn restraints against behaving aggressively.

At the Harvard University nursery school, Elliot Aronson and J. Merrill Carlsmith asked five-year-olds to rate the attractiveness of several toys, then forbade them to play with one of their favorites. For half the children the threat of punishment was mild—"I would be a little angry." For the other half it was more severe—the experimenter said he would not only be very angry but also would have to take all the toys away. The children were then left alone. Both threats were effective. All the children resisted the temptation to play with the forbidden toy.

Although both threats worked, the psychological mechanism involved was significantly different, as was shown when the children were again asked to rate the toys' attractiveness. The children who had been severely threatened still liked the forbidden toy. Some even found it more

Protesting against the Vietnam War, over 15,000 Americans mass before the Washington Monument in April 1965 at one of the earliest peace demonstrations. Bitterly opposed by the government at first, the antiwar demonstrations spread over much of the United States, Europe and Asia—providing generally peaceable pressure that helped to turn public opinion against the war and forced the government to withdraw from Vietnam.

desirable than before. But the mildly threatened children found the forbidden toy less attractive than before. This happened, Aronson concluded, for a seemingly perverse reason. The mild threat itself did not seem sufficient justification for giving up the toy. Lacking any strong external reason for not doing something they had previously found attractive, they had to make up a reason to justify their strange behavior in giving up the toy. "They succeeded in convincing themselves that they hadn't played with it because they didn't really like it."

A later study at Stanford University confirmed the role of internal justification in restraining prohibited conduct. Psychologist Jonathan Freedman provided young boys, aged seven to nine, with several toys and then forbade them to play with the most desirable one, a battery-powered robot. Half of the young subjects were severely threatened —"I'll be very angry and will have to do something about it." The rest received a very mild threat—"It is wrong to play with the robot."

Freedman then disappeared from the school and in a few weeks another experimenter showed up, someone who seemed to have no connection with the first experiment and ostensibly was present to administer some written tests. The subjects were allowed to play with the same toys again, but no mention was made of the previously taboo robot. The use of the robot was measured. Most of the children who had been severely threatened weeks before proceeded to play with the robot; the threat now had no meaning. But the overwhelming majority of those who had been only mildly threatened refused to have anything to do with the robot. They had created their own justification for not playing with it—either it was not much fun or it was wrong—and they stuck to this attitude for as long as nine weeks.

Freedman's finding fits neatly with studies showing that severe punishment tends to make children peaceable at home but aggressive when their parents are not around. Allowing children or adults to construct internal justifications for restraining aggression helps develop a conscience, the values of which do not depend upon the presence of police or other authorities to enforce them. The problem for parents and lawmakers is to know in a given situation what constitutes a mild yet effective punishment. If the threat is too mild, it may not prevent the unwanted behavior. If it is too severe, it does not prevent unwanted behavior over the long term. There is no need for the child to develop his own justification—and internal guidelines—for nonaggression, and he lacks the unconscious pressure that turns him from violence.

The internal guidelines instilled by reward and punishment seem to control not only the external expression of aggression but also its internal source, the emotion of anger. For if a person has learned nonviolent, rather than violent, responses to troublesome situations, those responses may reduce his anger and make him feel better. This extraordinary conclusion stems from some of the catharsis experiments of Jack Hokanson. Hokanson had shown that when an angered male subject hurt his tormentor, the physiological signs of arousal—such as increased blood pressure and heart rate—quickly subsided. But when Hokanson tried the same experiment on women, the results were surprisingly different. Like the men, the women were angered by a tormentor, then given the chance to retaliate against him by administering false electric shocks to him. But hurting him brought only a very slow decline in their physiological arousal. In fact, the physiological signs subsided much more rapidly when the women had the chance to meet their tormentor's aggression with a friendly response. Not aggressiveness but friendliness reduced their tension.

To Hokanson, this unforeseen result suggested that the tension-reducing effect of catharsis must be a learned reaction and not an instinctive one. People in general, he reasoned, try to learn to protect themselves against aggression from others. When they are successful in stopping the aggressor, they experience a sense of mental and physical relief. For a boy, the effective act may well be striking his tormentor. But girls are much more likely to learn a nonaggressive response such as talking soothingly to the aggressor, especially if the tormentor is a male. Thus, Hokanson concluded, the women in his experiment had experienced physical relief from their friendly responses because being friendly had proved successful at disarming tormentors in the past.

Hokanson tested his hypothesis that catharsis was learned with a succession of ingenious variations on his experiment. He rigged the tests of women so that a friendly response was not effective in stopping the tormentor's aggression. Counterattack was now the only means by which to stop the tormentor. After a while the women became conditioned by these changed conditions and they began to act like men, responding to arousal by hurting the tormentor. And, like men, when they met shock with shock they showed a reduction in tension.

Next Hokanson went back to male subjects and rigged the tests the opposite way—only a friendly response was effective in stopping the tormentor. This conditioned male subjects to react like women. Toward the end of the game, the men's arousal was reduced when they countered aggression with friendliness; they found physiological relief—catharsis—in friendly responses instead of aggressive ones.

Hokanson's intriguing experiments have several important implications, not all fully explored. For example, one test was set up so that subjects would deliver real, though mild, electric shocks to themselves in response to aggression. In a short time, they had learned to reduce physiological tension by hurting themselves. Hokanson believes that in roughly the same way a young child may learn to be masochistic. Hurting himself—physically or through self-deprecating remarks—could somehow serve to reduce his own tension when it is aroused by attack and teach him to meet future aggression with self-hurt. Hokanson's finding that catharsis is learned may also explain the extraordinarily nonaggressive behavior exhibited in certain cultures. People in those cultures may simply have learned that a nonaggressive response can be as effective a tension reducer as an aggressive one.

Among the most unusual experiments to probe the causes and possible cures for aggression are the elaborate ones set up by a husband-and-wife team of social psychologists then at the University of Oklahoma, Muzafer and Carolyn Sherif. Their studies are among the more controversial in a controversial field, for children were deliberately aroused to commit normally forbidden acts, an experience that —if other experiments can be believed—might seriously affect the subjects' behavior long after the experiment ended. Despite the questions raised by the methods, the results cannot be ignored; they offer startling insights into the causes of aggression—and possible cures.

At the time the Sherifs began their work, in 1949, it was widely believed that a principal cause of aggression between groups was differences such as race or religion. The Sherifs thought an equally significant influence might be provided by cultural values, particularly the beliefs in competition and self-advancement that are so fundamental in Western society. They determined to test one particular hypothesis: when one group can achieve its goals only at the expense of another, hostility is bound to result even though both groups are composed of similar, normally adjusted individuals. So they established summer camps for children, first in Connecticut and later in Oklahoma, to which they brought 11- and 12-year-old boys purposely selected for their homogeneous backgrounds—all came from stable, white, Protestant, middle-class homes. The members of the camp staff were all accomplices of the experimenters, and Sherif himself watched unobtrusively in his role as the caretaker, Mr. Mussee.

During the first experiment in Connecticut, the boys were given several days to form friendships. Then the experimenters broke up these friendships by separating the youngsters into two groups of about a

*Perhaps the most famous—and successful
—champion of nonviolence in modern
times was India's Mohandas K. Gandhi.
"Nonviolence," he preached, "is mightier
than the mightiest weapon of destruction"
—and he demonstrated the practicality
of his doctrine with the 32-year campaign
of passive resistance that won India
independence. Gandhi is shown here with
his spinning wheel, on which he spun
every day. It was no mere symbol, but an
economic weapon with which he exerted
pressure, getting Indians to make
their own cloth instead of buying imports.*

dozen each. The groups, which came to call themselves the Red Devils and the Bull Dogs, slept in different bunkhouses, ate at separate tables and participated in separate activities, such as hikes and swimming, that were designed to foster feelings of group solidarity.

Then a series of contests was arranged, bringing the Red Devils and the Bull Dogs into direct competition as teams. The teams could gain points for the performance of camp duties, such as cleaning their bunkhouses, as well as for winning athletic contests. The prize for each member of the winning team was a camping knife. At first, good sportsmanship prevailed. After the tug of war, for example, the winning Bull Dogs cheered for the losers and the Red Devils responded in kind.

As the competition progressed, however, the Red Devils fell further behind in the point standings, and frustrations mounted. Team cheers changed from "Two, four, six, eight, who do we appreciate" to "Two, four, six, eight, who do we appreci-hate." By the night of the Bull Dogs' final triumph, tempers had reached the boiling point on both sides. That night, to add to the frustrations, the experimenters played some dirty tricks. They staged a party, covertly messed up half of the cake and ice cream as if it had been battered in transit and then made sure the losing Red Devils got to the party first. The Red Devils quickly claimed all the best treats, of course, and when the Bull Dogs arrived to find only damaged goods, trouble started. The two groups traded insults and one of the Bull Dogs threateningly brandished his newly won camping knife. At lunch the next day, insults flew back and forth, then bits of food and even table knives and saucers. The rest of the day and into the night the Red Devils and the Bull Dogs engaged in sporadic warfare, using green apples for ammunition. When counselors tried to arrange a truce, one of them was threatened by a pair of belligerent Bull Dogs.

This stage of the experiment was abruptly terminated. It had convinced the researchers of the validity of their hypothesis about the role of competition in fostering aggression. Now they set out to explore ways of countering such arousal. They attempted to cool hostilities between the two warring groups with campwide activities that encouraged cooperation. None of these attempts worked very well until a competition was arranged between a team from a neighboring town and an all-star team of campers chosen by both groups. Faced with a common enemy, the Red Devils and Bull Dogs began to cooperate.

The threat posed by a common enemy, of course, is one of the oldest ways of controlling conflicts and group rivalries within a society. After World War II, for example, conflict with colonial powers enabled many of the emerging African nations to overcome tribal rivalries and achieve unity. Communist China appears to have maintained remarkable solidarity at home partly by conjuring up an external threat—first from the United States, then the Soviet Union.

To the summer-camp experimenters, this method of dampening hostility—inventing an external threat—was scarcely satisfactory. It was temporary (after the African nations achieved independence, several of them were wracked again by intertribal conflict). More important, it only created the potential for hostility on a larger scale—the entire camp pitted against an outside foe.

Five years later, the Sherifs tried a different tack. This time the camp was in an isolated area of Oklahoma, and the young subjects were taken there in two separate groups, called the Rattlers and the Eagles. Once more, the hostility generated by intergroup competition got out of hand. This time the Sherifs first tested the common belief that pleasant social contacts, such as going to the motion pictures together, would curb intergroup hostility. Such contacts only heightened tensions.

Then the Sherifs tried a different counter for hostility, which they called "superordinate goals." This approach was based on the proposition that, as Sherif put it, "just as competition generates friction, working in a common endeavor should promote harmony." To be effective, however, the common endeavor had to aim at a goal that appealed to all groups but was beyond the resources of any one group. A familiar example is the emergency created by flood, famine or fire that calls forth superhuman energy and cooperation.

The Sherifs created their own "natural" disasters. Mysteriously, the camp water supply broke down; members of both groups worked together to find the cause—stuffed faucets and a turned-off valve. On an overnight expedition, the food truck stalled; both groups literally had to pull together—on the same rope they had used a few days before in a fierce tug of war. Slowly, as the boys faced and solved these and other problems together, the bickering and name calling ebbed and cooperation increased. At the end of their stay at camp, the boys voted to go home on the same bus. On the way the Rattlers put up the money they had won in a fierce competition to buy refreshments for all.

The Sherifs' concept of superordinate goals was not really new. Consciously or unconsciously it has been applied to reduce tensions in spheres larger than a boys' camp—most recently in the joint Soviet-American efforts in space exploration. Their success, however limited, in improving cooperation between two powerfully competitive nations is one more indication aggression is not beyond human control.

Acknowledgments

The index for this book was prepared by Anita R. Beckerman. The author and editors of this book also wish to thank the following persons and institutions for their assistance: James A. Arey, New York City; Dr. William A. Belson, Survey Research Centre, London School of Economics and Political Science, London, England; Kerry Clemmons, Director of Development, Florida Ocean Sciences Institute, Deerfield Beach, Florida; John Cocchi, Boxoffice Magazine, New York; Celso Coppola, Director of Social Services, Juvenile Section, Ministry of Grace and Justice, Rome; Cécile Coutin, Curator, Musée des Deux Guerres Mondiales, Paris; Pierre Debuche, Director, *Loisirs Jeunes Magazine*, Paris; Enzo de Orsi, Director, Institute of Juvenile Re-Education, Eboli, Italy; Nancy DeVore, Anthro-Photo, Cambridge, Massachusetts; Paul Ekman, Professor of Psychology, University of California at San Francisco; William K. Everson, Department of Cinema Studies, New York University, New York City; Franco Ferracuti, Professor of Criminologic Medicine and Forensic Psychiatry, Faculty of Medicine, Rome University, Rome; Robert Gardner, Cambridge, Massachusetts; Heribert Heinrichs, Director, Audio-Visual Center, University of Hildesheim, West Germany; Malcolm Kirk, New York City; Alf McCreary, Belfast, Ireland; Loren A. McIntyre, Arlington, Virginia; Irving H. Phillips Jr., Baltimore, Maryland; Tom Picton, London; Victoria Reiss, Organizer, Parents for Responsibility in the Toy Industry, New York City; Robert Rosof, President, Florida Ocean Sciences Institute, Deerfield Beach, Florida; Stanley Schachter, Professor of Psychology, Columbia University, New York City; Giovanna Scherillo, Magistrate, Ministry of Grace and Justice, Rome; Ian Taylor, Centre for Criminological Studies, University of Sheffield, England; Kathleen Webber, Librarian, Highway Safety Research Institute, The University of Michigan at Ann Arbor; Edward O. Wilson, Professor of Zoology, Harvard University, Cambridge, Massachusetts.

Bibliography

Arey, James A., *The Sky Pirates*. Charles Scribner's Sons, 1972.

Arnold, William J., and David Levine, eds., *Nebraska Symposium on Motivation*. University of Nebraska Press, 1969.

Aronson, Elliot, *The Social Animal*. W. H. Freeman and Company, 1972.

Bandura, Albert, *Aggression: A Social Learning Analysis*. Prentice-Hall, Inc., 1973.

Bandura, Albert, and Richard Walters, *Social Learning and Personality Development*. Holt, Rinehart & Winston, Inc., 1963.

Beals, Alan R., et al., *Culture in Process*. Holt, Rinehart & Winston, Inc., 1967.

Berkowitz, Leonard:
Aggression: A Social Psychological Analysis. McGraw-Hill Book Company, Inc., 1962.
Roots of Aggression. Atherton Press, 1969.
A Survey of Social Psychology. The Dryden Press, Inc., 1972.

Brady, Robert A., *The Spirit and Structure of German Fascism*. The Viking Press, 1937.

Bramson, Leon, and George W. Goethals, eds., *War*. Basic Books, Inc., 1968.

Cater, Douglass, and Stephen Strickland, *TV Violence and the Child*. Russell Sage Foundation, 1975.

Chagnon, Napoleon A., *Yanomamö: The Fierce People*. Holt, Rinehart & Winston, Inc., 1968.

Clark, Ramsey, *Crime in America*. Simon and Schuster, Inc., 1970.

Cline, Victor B., ed., *Where Do You Draw the Line?* Brigham Young University Press, 1974.

Conrad, Jack, *The Many Worlds of Man*. Thomas Y. Crowell Company, 1964.

Crump, Spencer, *Black Riot in Los Angeles*. Trans-Anglo Books, 1966.

Dentan, Robert Knox, *The Semai*. Holt, Rinehart & Winston, 1968.

De Vore, Irven, ed., *Primate Behavior: Field Studies of Monkeys and Apes*. Holt, Rinehart & Winston, 1965.

Doob, Anthony N., and Dennis T. Regan, eds., *Readings in Experimental Social Psychology*. Appleton-Century-Crofts, 1971.

Ekman, Paul, and Wallace V. Friesen, *Unmasking the Face*. Prentice-Hall, Inc., 1975.

Eron, Leonard D., et al., *Learning of Aggression in Children*. Little, Brown & Co., 1971.

Everson, William K., *Pictorial History of the Western Film*. Citadel Press, Inc., 1971.

Freedman, Jonathan L., et al., *Social Psychology*. Prentice-Hall, Inc., 1970.

Freedman, Jonathan L., and Anthony N. Doob, *Deviancy*. Academic Press, Inc., 1969.

Freedman, Jonathan L., J. Merrill Carlsmith and David O. Sears, *Social Psychology*. Prentice-Hall, Inc., 1970.

Gunn, John, *Violence*. Praeger Publishers, 1973.

Hubbard, David G., M.D., *The Skyjacker: His Flights of Fantasy*. The Macmillan Company, 1971.

Jacobs, Paul, *Prelude to Riot: A View of Urban America from the Bottom*. Random House, 1966.

Johnson, Roger N., *Aggression in Man and Animals*. W. B. Saunders Company, 1972.

Knollenberg, Bernhard, *Growth of the American Revolution 1766-1775*. The Free Press, 1975.

Krupat, Edward, ed., *Psychology is Social*. Scott, Foresman and Company, 1975.

Latané, Bibb, and John M. Darley, *The Unresponsive Bystander: Why Doesn't He Help?* Appleton-Century-Crofts, 1970.

Lifton, Robert J., *Home from the War*. Simon & Schuster, Inc., 1973.

Limpkin, Clive, *Northern Ireland: The Battle of Bogside*. Penguin Books Ltd., 1972.

Lorenz, Konrad, *On Aggression*. Bantam Books, 1971.

MacCoby, Eleanor, and Carol N. Jacklin,

The Psychology of Sex Differences. Stanford University Press, 1974.

Mansbach, Richard W., ed., *Northern Ireland: Half Century of Partition.* Facts on File, Inc., 1973.

Maple, Terry, and Douglas Matheson, eds., *Aggression, Hostility and Violence . . . Nature or Nurture?* Holt, Rinehart & Winston, Inc., 1973.

Megargee, Edwin I., and Jack E. Hokanson, *The Dynamics of Aggression.* Harper & Row, Publishers, 1970.

Milgram, Stanley, *Obedience to Authority.* Harper & Row, Publishers, 1974.

Montagu, Ashley, *Man and Aggression.* Oxford University Press, 1973.

Ng, Larry, ed., *Alternatives to Violence.* TIME-LIFE BOOKS, 1968.

Pines, Maya, *The Brain Changers: Scientists and the New Mind Control.* Harcourt Brace Jovanovich, Inc., 1973.

Scherer, Klaus R., Ronald P. Abeles and Claude S. Fischer, *Human Aggression and Conflict.* Prentice-Hall, Inc., 1975.

Seale, Patrick, and Maureen McConville, *Red Flag/Black Flag: French Revolution 1968.* G. P. Putnam's Sons, 1968.

Sherif, Muzafer, et al., *Intergroup Conflict and Cooperation: The Robbers Cave Experiment.* Institute of Group Relations, The University of Oklahoma, 1961.

Sherif, Muzafer and Carolyn W., *Groups in Harmony and Tension.* Octagon Books, 1973.

Simpson, George E., and J. Milton Yinger, *Racial and Cultural Minorities.* Harper & Row, 1965.

Singer, Jerome L., ed., *The Control of Aggression and Violence.* Academic Press, Inc., 1971.

Tiger, Lionel, *Men in Groups.* Vintage Books, 1970.

U.S. Federal Bureau of Investigation, *Crime in the United States: 1974 Uniform Crime Reports.* Issued by Clarence M. Kelley, 1974.

Van Voris, W. H., *Violence in Ulster.* University of Massachusetts Press, 1975.

Wilson, Edward, *Sociobiology.* The Belknap Press of Harvard University Press, 1975.

Zobel, Hiller B., *The Boston Massacre.* W. W. Norton & Company, Inc., 1970.

Picture Credits

Index

Numerals in italics indicate a photograph or drawing of the subject mentioned.

violence; Western movies
Chromosome, extra, and criminal behavior, 13
Civil rights demonstration, *86*, 137. *See also* Nonviolence
Cline, Victor, on effects of television violence, 68
Competition, and aggression, 151-152, 165, 168
Conditioning, learning aggressive behavior through: effect of family atmosphere on decision to serve or not to serve in armed forces, 60; rewards and punishment, 44-45, 51-56, 60; television, 60-61, 64-65, 68-69. *See also* Rewards and punishment; Television violence
Conformity, in the group, 122-123, 126
Constructive behavior, 160-161
Contagion of violence, 99, 101; and airplane hijackings, *100*, 101; effects of telegraph and television on, 99, 101; and kidnapings, *100*, 101
Control of aggression, 145, 156-169; appeasement, 22-23, 157-159; behavior-modification techniques at Florida Ocean Sciences Institute, *153-155*; common enemy in, 168-169; cooling-off time, 156-157; and doctrines of nonviolence, 159-160, *166-167*; and John Lindsay's walking tour of Harlem ghetto, *158*; and love-oriented techniques, 160; and peace demonstrations, *162*; and punishment, 161-163; role of mind in, 159; and sex differences in response to troublesome situations, 164; stressing constructive behavior, 160-161; superordinate goals in, 169; and threats of punishment, 161-163
Cooling-off time, 156-157
Crimes, violent: in foreign cities, 9; in Great Britain, 44; increase in, 9; in United States, 9, 44, 101, *102. See also* Homicide
Crowding, and aggression, 91

D
Darley, John, on anonymity and reaction to violence, 113, 114-115
Darwin, Charles, on violence and the evolution of animals, 13
Darwinism, Social, 13
Davitz, Joel, on stressing constructive behavior, 160-161

Dehumanization: abusive labels used in, 128, 130; and blame-the-victim syndrome, 130-131; and group violence, 128, 130; Hitler's use of, 128; pejorative stereotypes as forms of, 130
Deindividuation, 110, *114*, 138; experiments on anonymity and aggression, 111, 113. *See also* Anonymity
Delgado, José, brain stimulation experiments of, 30
Delinquents, rehabilitation of, *153-155*
Demolition derby, *40-41*
Dentan, Robert, on learned violence, 48
Deviant behavior: fear of, in groups, 122-123; long hair and, 122-123
Displacement of aggression, 17, 106-107; depicted in cartoon, 24, *25*; lynching as, 107
Dissonance theory, 131, 140
Dollard, John, on scarcity of jobs and aggression against German immigrants, 128
Dominance: and animal aggression, 19, 22; and inhibitions against deadly violence, 22-23
Doob, Anthony: on aggression-reducing effect of physical violence, 147, 149; on deviance, 123; on sex of target of aggression, 106

E
Ebbesen, Ebbe B., on verbal aggression, 149-150
Eichmann, Adolf, 117, *118*
Einstein, Albert, 17
Ellsworth, Phoebe, experiments on staring, 89, 91
Emotional aggression, 12
Eron, Leonard, on television violence and aggressiveness in children, 47-48
Executions, diffusion of responsibility in, 110
Experiments for measurement of aggression, 8

F
Fear, and television violence, 9
Festinger, Leon, dissonance theory of, 131, 140
Fighting: J. P. Scott on, 30-31; parental praise for, 56; and plaudits of peers, *54*, 56
Finland, homicide rates in, *16*
Florida Ocean Sciences Institute,

behavior-modification techniques at, *153-155*
France, national strike in (1968), 94, 99
Freedman, Jonathan: on deindividuation and group aggression, 110; on deviance, 123; on threats of punishment, 163
Freud, Sigmund: on outlets for aggression, 17, 145; on reasons for aggression, 15, 17
Frustration leading to aggression, 90-94; accessibility of the goal and, 93-94; arising from competition for resources, 127-128; prejudice and, 126-127; and railway commuters in Rio de Janeiro, 91-92; revolutions and, 94; among shoppers in German store, *90;* at supermarket checkout counter, 93

G
Gandhi, Mohandas K., 159, *166-167*
Genetic defects and aggression, 13
Germany: dehumanization of Jews, 128; television violence in, 61, 64
Goals, superordinate, to produce harmony, 169
Great Britain: caning in English schools, 55; lack of violence in, 44, 55; motor vehicle fatalities in, 103; news programs edited for viewing by children in, 68; soccer fans' hooliganism in, *95-98*, 152; television violence in, 61
Grimms' *Fairy Tales*, violence in, *57-59;* impact of, 57
Gross, Alan E., on sex of target of aggression, 106
Group(s): and bystanders' refusal to intervene on behalf of people in distress, 113-114, *116*; and committing violence for a higher cause than personal reasons, 115, 117, *118*, 119; conformity in, 122-123, 126; factors increasing likelihood of violence in, 109-110; fear of being labeled deviant in, 122-123. *See also* Anonymity; Group aggression
Group aggression, 12, 108-143; blame-the-victim syndrome and, 120-121; at Boston Massacre, 109; at civil rights demonstration, *86;* at confrontation at Kent State University, 130-131; dehumanization and, 128, 130; deindividuation and, 110-111, 113, *114*, 138; deviance and, 122-123;

frustrations and, 94, 127-128; and Hatfield-McCoy feud, *112*; Hitler's role in, 128; incited by use of posters, *124-125*, 128; and Japanese students, *108*, 109; and lynching, 107, *120-121*; at My Lai, 122; and obedience to authority, 115, 117, *118*, 119; prejudice as cause of, 126-127, 134; and slaughter of six million Jews during World War II, 117, 118, 128; and soccer hooliganism, British, *95-98*, 152; by street gangs, *129*; and violence in Northern Ireland, *132-143*. *See also* Anonymity; Dehumanization; Group(s); Northern Ireland, violence in; Obedience to authority; Prejudice

Guns: easy accessibility of, in the United States, 101, *102*; effect of, on level of aggression of aroused people, 101-103

H

Hall, Edward T., on need for psychological elbow room, 91

Hammett, Van Buren, on automobile as weapon of aggression, 103

Hara-kiri, 20

Harris, Mary, on frustration and accessibility of goal, 93

Hartmann, Donald, on spectator violence, 156

Hatfield-McCoy feud, *112*

Hicks, David J., on long-range effect of learned aggression, 47

Hijackings, airplane. *See* Airplane hijackings

Hitler, Adolf, 128

Hockey, 151

Hokanson, Jack E.: on committing aggression and reducing tension, 146-147; on learned responses to troublesome situations, 164-165

Homicide: during prosperous times and bad times, 93-94; and easy accessibility of guns in the United States, 101, *102*; rates of, in selected countries, *16*

Hopi Indians, behavior of, 43-44

Hydraulic model of aggression, 23, 27

I

Imitation, learning aggressive behavior through, 44, 45-49, 51

Infanticide, sex-biased, 43

Innate aggression, 15, 17-19, 22-23

Instrumental aggression, 12; and loyal obedience to the group, 12

Ireland, Northern. *See* Northern Ireland

Italy, self-mutilation or self-flogging by Christian penitents of, 35

J

James, Jesse, 8

James, William, on causes of aggression, 15

Japan: homicide rates in, 16; special television news program for children in, 68-69; television-viewing in, 61

Japanese violence, 15; in *Forty-Seven Ronin*, 20; and hara-kiri, 20; and mass purification rite of youths, *32-33*; paradox of, *20-21*; and ritualized assassination, *20-21*; between students and police, *108*, 109; on television, 64

K

Kahn, Michael, on verbal aggression, 150

Kent State University: blame-the-victim syndrome among townspeople, 131; confrontation at, 130-131

Kidnapings: in Argentina, 101; contagion of violence and, 100, 101

King, Martin Luther, Jr., 159

L

Latané, Bibb, on anonymity and reaction to violence, 113, 114-115

Learning aggression, 42-81; in adulthood, 49, 51; and Bobo doll experiments by Albert Bandura, 45, *46*, 47, 51-52; through conditioning, 44-45, 51-56, 60; effectiveness of models in, 48-49, 51; and Grimms' *Fairy Tales*, *57-59*; through imitation, 44, 45-49, 51; inside and outside of the home, 45; long-range effects of, 47; movies and, 60-61; and Semai tribe of central Malaya, *48*; television and, *42*, 45, 47-48; and violence in military training, 49; and violent toys, *66-67*; and *waiteri* of Yanomamö tribesmen of Venezuela, 43. *See also* Rewards and punishment; Television violence; Western movies

Lifton, Robert Jay, on feelings of guilt related to proximity of subject and victim, 119

Lindsay, John, and walking tour of Harlem ghetto, *158*

Lombroso, Cesare, 13

Lorenz, Konrad: *On Aggression*, 17; on functions of animal aggression, 18-19;

hydraulic model of aggression, 23; on weapons and human violence, 23. *See also* Animal aggression

Lowen, Alexander, on ventilative therapies, 150-151

Lynchings, *120-121*; as displacement, 107; economic frustration and, 107, 121; frequency of, 107

M

McDougall, William, on the instinct of pugnacity, 15

Menninger, Karl, on violence, 7-8

Mexico, homicide rates in, *16*

Milgram, Stanley: "Eichmann Experiment" conducted by, 117-118; *Obedience to Authority*, 118-119

Military training, violent models in, 49

Movies, 60-61; effect of, on aggressiveness of children, 71; Western, *70-81*. *See also* Television violence; Western movies

Murder. *See* Homicide

My Lai, behavior of American soldiers at, 122

N

Newspapers: emphasis on violence and sex in, *14*; learning about violence from, 45; publicity in, about street gangs, 56

Nonviolence, 159-160, *166-167*; Martin Luther King Jr. and, 159; Mohandas K. Gandhi and, 159, *166-167*; rewards for, 160; self-control in, 159-160

Northern Ireland, violence in, *132-143*; Bloody Sunday killings and, *137*, 138; deindividuation and, *138*; dissonance theory and, 140; participation of children in, *142-143*; prejudice and discrimination as cause of, 134; Roman Catholic civil rights demonstrations in, 137

Norway, homicide rates in, *16*

O

Obedience: to authority, 115, 117, *118*, 119, 120; Adolf Eichmann on German slaughter of six million Jews, 117, *118*; "Eichmann Experiment" conducted by Stanley Milgram, 117-118; level of, related to proximity of subject and victim, 119; organized warfare and, 115, 117; posters and, *124*; terrorist

television, 9; weapons and, 23, 101-103, 105. *See also* Aggression; Group violence; Television violence

Violence profile, television, 61. *See also* Television violence

Violent crimes. *See* Crimes, violent; Homicide

Von Bernhardi, Friedrich, on warfare, 13

W

Warfare, organized, 8, 13, 31; and behavior of American soldiers at My Lai, 122; and effect of family atmosphere on decision to serve or not to serve, 60; and feelings of guilt related to proximity of subject and victim, 119; and obedience to authority, 115, 117; peace demonstrations against, *162*; posters inciting aggression, *124-125*

Warfare, sham, 33, *38*, 50, 146

Weapons, 23, 101-103, 105; automobiles as, 83, 103, 105; and easy accessibility of guns in the United States, 101, *102*; as probable cause of aggression, 101, 103

Weather, bad, and aggression, 87-88

Western movies, *70-81*; change in attitude toward women in, *77*; and early silent films, *72-73*; effect of, on aggressiveness of children, 71; and lack of blood in films of the 1940s, *74-75*; and violence of bloody massacre in *The Wild Bunch*, *80-81*; and violence in films produced after World War II, *76-77*; and violence in Italian (spaghetti) Westerns, *78-79*

Whitman, Charles, 13

Wilson, Edward O., on animal aggression, 26, 28

Y

Yablonsky, Lewis, on violence of street gangs, 129

Yanomamö tribe of Venezuela, 43

Z

Zillmann, Dolf: on arousal and aggression, 85; on words of explanation, 159

Zimbardo, Philip, on anonymity and aggression, 111, 113